RURAL

W9-DGT-166

AMERICA

**edited by SUZANNE FREMON
and MORROW WILSON**

THE REFERENCE SHELF

Volume 48   Number 3

THE H. W. WILSON COMPANY

New York   1976

THE REFERENCE SHELF

The books in this series contain reprints of articles, excerpts
n books, and addresses on current issues and social trends in the
ited States and other countries. There are six separately bound
nbers in each volume, all of which are generally published
the same calendar year. One number is a collection of recent
eches; each of the others is devoted to a single subject and
es background information and discussion from various points
view, concluding with a comprehensive bibliography. Books
in the series may be purchased individually or on subscription.

Copyright © 1976
By The H. W. Wilson Company
PRINTED IN THE UNITED STATES OF AMERICA

Library of Congress Cataloging in Publication Data
Main entry under title:
Rural America.

  (The Reference shelf ; v. 48, no. 3)
Bibliography: p.
  CONTENTS: *The nineteenth century picture*: De Tocqueville, A. The American wilderness. De Tocqueville, A. Life in
the wilderness. Thoreau, H. D. Experiment in homesteading.
Twain, M. Growing up in Missouri. Twain, M. Mississippi River
pilots. Moore, T. E. Peddlers. Rourke, C. Traveling players. Garland, H. Life on an Iowa farm. Opening up Oklahoma. *The
twentieth century picture*: Wilson, C. M. American peasants.
Wilson, C. M. Law makers and breakers. Allen, F. L. When the
farms blew away. Lerner, M. The way of the farmer. Lerner, M.
The decline of the small town. Brogan, D. W. Political influence
of the farm bloc. Black, R. C. The American farmer . . . our first
"hybrid." Walsh, J. U.S. agribusiness and agricultural trends.
Shifting patterns in rural areas: Ellis, W. N. The new ruralism:
the post-industrial age is upon us. Logsdon, G. The keys to homesteading success. Nordheimer, J. America's rural poor: the picture
is changing. Terkel, S. Working the land. Terkel, S. Second
chance: Fred Ringley

  1. United States—Rural conditions—Addresses, essays, lectures.
2. Country life—United States—History—Addresses, essays, lectures.
I. Fremon, Suzanne. II. Wilson, Morrow. III. Series.
HN57.R78   301.35′0973   76-21771
ISBN 0-8242-0597-9

PREFACE

There has always been a compelling mythic quality about living close to and working the land that has persisted in spite of the hardships and difficulties of that life in reality. It is important, therefore, to try to sort the facts from the fantasy.

This volume contains many different kinds of writing on rural life, from many different points of view ranging over two hundred years, beginning with Alexis de Tocqueville's view in the nineteenth century of life in the wilderness and ending with practical advice written in 1975 for those who want to go back to the land from the cities. The compilation consists of three major sections, which take us through the nineteenth century and the twentieth to America's bicentennial year.

In order to understand the situation in present-day rural America it is necessary to examine the traditions, conditions, and attitudes of the last century. Most of the articles in the first section are contemporary accounts of life in the nineteenth century; those by Alexis de Tocqueville, Thoreau, and Mark Twain are classics. The nineteenth century was a time when the earlier potential for individual and national development was being realized. Rural life was extremely difficult, but the Jeffersonian ideal of economic independence, self-sufficiency, personal freedom, and unlimited opportunity seemed within reach because of the unlimited land and the natural resources that were there for the taking. In his *Notes on Virginia*, Jefferson expressed the basis for his social and political agrarianism:

Those who labor in the earth are the chosen people of God, if ever He had a chosen people, whose breasts He has made His peculiar deposit for substantial and genuine virtue. It is the focus in which He keeps alive that sacred fire, which otherwise might escape from the face of the earth. Corruption of morals in the mass of cultivators is a phenomenon of which no age nor nation has furnished an example. It is the mark set on those, who, not looking up to heaven, to their own soil and industry, as does the husbandman, for their subsistence, depend for it on casualties and caprice of customers. Dependence begets subservience and venality, suffocates the germ of virtue, and prepares fit tools for the designs of ambition.

Throughout the nineteenth century the conflict between the drive to move on, to better one's life, and the need for stability inherent in the very nature of farm life and rural settlement is apparent. The situation in the twentieth century is vastly different. Urbanization, industrialization, and a huge increase in population shifting towards the cities, have supplanted the original American dream, which always included the possibility of moving on to new, unsettled lands farther west if a farm did not prosper or a place became too crowded. But the dream has persisted in spite of the split between the myth of the simple, tilling-the-soil, independent life and the reality of rural hardship that still exists for many in spite of the application of modern technology to farming. Indeed, some of the most lyrical writing of the twentieth century concerns country living. And so the dream persisted, bringing periodic back-to-the-land movements, throughout this century in spite of the evolution of farming as big business.

These contrasts, the drifts and changes that appear to embody an irreversible trend, are the subject of the last section of this book. The economic situation and the recognition of the importance of psychic needs have brought a renewed interest in homesteading in the face of what seemed to be an inevitable takeover of the rural scene by agribusiness. The picture of America's rural poor is also changing.

Perhaps these new developments will eventually produce a better mix, closer to the early American rural scene and the character of America's early years.

The editors wish to thank the authors and publishers who have granted permission to reprint the materials which make up this volume.

SUZANNE FREMON AND MORROW WILSON

July 1976

CONTENTS

I. THE NINETEENTH CENTURY PICTURE

EDITORS' INTRODUCTION

The American nineteenth century was an optimistic time, when earlier potential was being realized. The Jeffersonian ideal of the economic independence, personal freedom, and unlimited opportunity of those who tilled the soil was in many respects a reality, partially as a result of unlimited land and natural resources. This was one of the observations of Alexis de Tocqueville, the French statesman and political philosopher, who traveled extensively in the United States during the 1830s and examined the conditions and institutions that contributed to American democracy. Portions from his essays make up the first two articles in this section.

The American writer and social critic Henry David Thoreau actually lived an experiment in solitary homesteading. *Walden,* his treatise on the subject (excerpts from which comprise the second article), is one of the most famous pieces of writing in all literature about rural living and its social implications. Mark Twain's autobiographical account of growing up in mid-nineteenth-century mid-America makes up the fourth and fifth selections.

The next two articles are relatively modern accounts of two little-known aspects of American rural life in the last century. Truman Moore writes about the peddler, the forerunner of the present-day traveling salesman. This peculiarly American character embodied commercial virtues that are prized in our culture—initiative, perseverance, and a willingness to take risks and move around. He did not need family status, education, or substantial capital and so peddling could be one avenue of upward mobility, another phenomenon unique to classless American society in the eighteenth and nineteenth centuries.

9

Excerpts from Constance Rourke's account of traveling theatrical companies comprise the seventh article in this section. This and the previously mentioned selection are about people who were constantly on the move, in contrast to the farmers and townspeople who exemplified the more settled nature of farming and rural community life. However, as de Tocqueville observed, it is typical of all Americans, including farmers, to move on, or at least always to entertain the possibility of doing so. Perhaps, for that reason, peddlers and actors, along with other varieties of wanderers, were considered glamorous and exciting, though distrusted by the rural people to whom they offered their wares or talents.

The last two articles in this section, written in 1877 and 1889 respectively, again show the contrast between settling and moving. The first, from Hamlin Garland's *A Son of the Middle Border,* describes growing up on a farm in Iowa, when mechanization of agriculture was first beginning. The second is a newspaper account of the Oklahoma Land Run, staged when the United States government allowed white settlers to claim Cherokee land in Oklahoma.

THE AMERICAN WILDERNESS [1]

The chief circumstance which has favored the establishment and the maintenance of a democratic republic in the United States is the nature of the territory that the Americans inhabit. Their ancestors gave them the love of equality and of freedom; but God himself gave them the means of remaining equal and free, by placing them upon a boundless continent. General prosperity is favorable to the stability of all governments, but more particularly of a democratic one, which depends upon the will of the majority, and especially upon the will of that portion of the community which is

[1] Text from *Democracy in America*, by Alexis de Tocqueville (1805–1859), French writer, political philosopher, and government official. Knopf. '45. 2v. v 1, p 290–6. Copyright © 1945, renewed 1973, by Alfred A. Knopf, Inc. Reprinted by permission of the publisher.

most exposed to want. When the people rule, they must be rendered happy or they will overturn the state; and misery stimulates them to those excesses to which ambition rouses kings. The physical causes, independent of the laws, which promote general prosperity are more numerous in America than they ever have been in any other country in the world, at any other period of history. In the United States not only is legislation democratic, but Nature herself favors the cause of the people.

In what part of human history can be found anything similar to what is passing before our eyes in North America? The celebrated communities of antiquity were all founded in the midst of hostile nations, which they were obliged to subjugate before they could flourish in their place. Even the moderns have found, in some parts of South America, vast regions inhabited by a people of inferior civilization, who nevertheless had already occupied and cultivated the soil. To found their new states it was necessary to extirpate or subdue a numerous population, and they made civilization blush for its own success. But North America was inhabited only by wandering tribes, who had no thought of profiting by the natural riches of the soil; that vast country was still, properly speaking, an empty continent, a desert land awaiting its inhabitants.

Everything is extraordinary in America, the social condition of the inhabitants as well as the laws; but the soil upon which these institutions are founded is more extraordinary than all the rest. When the earth was given to men by the Creator, the earth was inexhaustible; but men were weak and ignorant, and when they had learned to take advantage of the treasures which it contained, they already covered its surface and were soon obliged to earn by the sword an asylum for repose and freedom. Just then North America was discovered, as if it had been kept in reserve by the Deity and had just risen from beneath the waters of the Deluge.

That continent still presents, as it did in the primeval

time, rivers that rise from never failing sources, green and moist solitudes, and limitless fields which the plowshare of the husbandman has never turned. In this state it is offered to man, not barbarous, ignorant, and isolated, as he was in the early ages, but already in possession of the most important secrets of nature, united to his fellow men, and instructed by the experience of fifty centuries. At this very time thirteen millions of civilized Europeans are peaceably spreading over those fertile plains, with whose resources and extent they are not yet themselves accurately acquainted. Three or four thousand soldiers drive before them the wandering races of the aborigines; these are followed by the pioneers, who pierce the woods, scare off the beasts of prey, explore the courses of the inland streams, and make ready the triumphal march of civilization across the desert.

Often, in the course of this work, I have alluded to the favorable influence of the material prosperity of America upon the institutions of that country. This reason had already been given by many others before me, and is the only one which, being palpable to the senses, as it were, is familiar to Europeans. I shall not, then, enlarge upon a subject so often handled and so well understood, beyond the addition of a few facts. An erroneous notion is generally entertained that the deserts of America are peopled by European emigrants who annually disembark upon the coasts of the New World, while the American population increase and multiply upon the soil which their forefathers tilled. The European settler usually arrives in the United States without friends and often without resources; in order to subsist, he is obliged to work for hire, and he rarely proceeds beyond that belt of industrious population which adjoins the ocean. The desert cannot be explored without capital or credit; and the body must be accustomed to the rigors of a new climate before it can be exposed in the midst of the forest. It is the Americans themselves who daily quit the spots which gave them birth, to acquire extensive do-

mains in a remote region. Thus the European leaves his
cottage for the transatlantic shores, and the American, who
is born on that very coast, plunges in his turn into the wilds
of central America. This double emigration is incessant; it
begins in the middle of Europe, it crosses the Atlantic
Ocean, and it advances over the solitudes of the New World.
Millions of men are marching at once towards the same
horizon; their language, their religion, their manners differ;
their object is the same. Fortune has been promised to them
somewhere in the West, and to the West they go to find it.

No event can be compared with this continuous removal
of the human race, except perhaps those irruptions which
caused the fall of the Roman Empire. Then, as well as now,
crowds of men were impelled in the same direction, to meet
and struggle on the same spot; but the designs of Providence
were not the same. Then every newcomer brought with him
destruction and death; now each one brings the elements of
prosperity and life. The future still conceals from us the
remote consequences of this migration of the Americans
towards the West; but we can readily apprehend its immediate results. As a portion of the inhabitants annually leave
the states in which they were born, the population of these
states increases very slowly, although they have long been
established. Thus in Connecticut, which yet contains only
fifty-nine inhabitants to the square mile, the population
has not been increased by more than one quarter in forty
years, while that of England has been augmented by one
third in the same period. The European emigrant always
lands, therefore, in a country that is but half full, and where
hands are in demand; he becomes a workman in easy circumstances, his son goes to seek his fortune in unpeopled
regions and becomes a rich landowner. The former amasses
the capital which the latter invests; and the stranger as well
as the native is unacquainted with want.

The laws of the United States are extremely favorable
to the division of property; but a cause more powerful than

the laws prevents property from being divided to excess. This is very perceptible in the states which are at last beginning to be thickly peopled. Massachusetts is the most populous part of the Union, but it contains only eighty inhabitants to the square mile, which is much less than in France, where one hundred and sixty-two are reckoned to the same extent of country. But in Massachusetts estates are very rarely divided; the eldest son generally takes the land, and the others go to seek their fortune in the wilderness. The law has abolished the right of primogeniture, but circumstances have concurred to reestablish it under a form of which none can complain and by which no just rights are impaired.

A single fact will suffice to show the prodigious number of individuals who thus leave New England to settle in the wilds. We were assured in 1830 that thirty-six of the members of Congress were born in the little state of Connecticut. The population of Connecticut, which constitutes only one forty-third part of that of the United States, thus furnished one eighth of the whole body of representatives. The state of Connecticut of itself, however, sends only five delegates to Congress; and the thirty-one others sit for the new Western states. If these thirty-one individuals had remained in Connecticut, it is probable that, instead of becoming rich landowners, they would have remained humble laborers, that they would have lived in obscurity without being able to rise into public life, and that, far from becoming useful legislators, they might have been unruly citizens.

These reflections do not escape the observation of the Americans any more than of ourselves.

It cannot be doubted [says Chancellor Kent, in his *Treatise on American Law* (v 4, p 580)] that the division of landed estates must produce great evils, when it is carried to such excess as that each parcel of land is insufficient to support a family; but these disadvantages have never been felt in the United States, and many generations must elapse before they can be felt. The extent of our inhabited territory, the abundance of adjacent land, and the continual stream of emigration flowing from the shores of the Atlantic towards the interior of the country, suffice as yet, and will long suffice, to prevent the parcelling out of estates.

It would be difficult to describe the avidity with which the American rushes forward to secure this immense booty that fortune offers. In the pursuit he fearlessly braves the arrow of the Indian and the diseases of the forest; he is un-impressed by the silence of the woods; the approach of beasts of prey does not disturb him, for he is goaded onwards by a passion stronger than the love of life. Before him lies a boundless continent, and he urges onward as if time pressed and he was afraid of finding no room for his exertions. I have spoken of the emigration from the older states, but how shall I describe that which takes place from the more recent ones? Fifty years have scarcely elapsed since Ohio was founded; the greater part of its inhabitants were not born within its confines; its capital has been built only thirty years, and its territory is still covered by an immense extent of uncultivated fields; yet already the population of Ohio is proceeding westward, and most of the settlers who descend to the fertile prairies of Illinois are citizens of Ohio. These men left their first country to improve their condition; they quit their second to ameliorate it still more; fortune awaits them everywhere, but not happiness. The desire of pros-perity has become an ardent and restless passion in their minds, which grows by what it feeds on. They early broke the ties that bound them to their natal earth, and they have contracted no fresh ones on their way. Emigration was at first necessary to them; and it soon becomes a sort of game of chance, which they pursue for the emotions it excites as much as for the gain it procures.

Sometimes the progress of man is so rapid that the desert reappears behind him. The woods stoop to give him a pas-sage, and spring up again when he is past. It is not uncom-mon, in crossing the new states of the West, to meet with deserted dwellings in the midst of the wilds; the traveler frequently discovers the vestiges of a log house in the most solitary retreat, which bear witness to the power, and no less to the inconstancy, of man. In these abandoned fields and over these ruins of a day the primeval forest soon scatters a fresh vegetation; the beasts resume the haunts which were once their own; and Nature comes smiling to cover the traces of man with green branches and flowers, which obliterate his ephemeral track.

I remember that in crossing one of the woodland districts which still cover the state of New York, I reached the shores of a lake which was embosomed in forests coeval with the world. A small island, covered with woods whose thick foliage concealed its banks, rose from the center of the waters. Upon the shores of the lake no object attested the presence of man except a column of smoke which might be seen on the horizon rising from the tops of the trees to the clouds and seeming to hang from heaven rather than to be mounting to it. An Indian canoe was hauled up on the sand, which tempted me to visit the islet that had first attracted my attention, and in a few minutes I set foot upon its banks. The whole island formed one of those delightful solitudes of the New World, which almost led civilized man to regret the haunts of the savage. A luxuriant vegetation bore witness to the incomparable fruitfulness of the soil. The deep silence, which is common to the wilds of North America, was broken only by the monotonous cooing of the wood-pigeons and the tapping of the woodpecker on the bark of trees. I was far from supposing that this spot had ever been inhabited, so completely did Nature seem to be left to herself; but when I reached the center of the isle, I thought that I discovered some traces of man. I then proceeded to examine the surrounding objects with care, and I soon perceived that a European had undoubtedly been led to seek a refuge in this place. Yet what changes had taken place in the scene of his labors! The logs which he had hastily hewn to build himself a shed had sprouted afresh; the very props were intertwined with living verdure, and his cabin was transformed into a bower. In the midst of these shrubs a few stones were to be seen, blackened with fire and sprinkled with thin ashes; here the hearth had no doubt been, and the chimney in falling had covered it with rubbish. I stood for some time in silent admiration of the resources of Nature and the littleness of man; and when I was obliged to leave that enchanting solitude, I exclaimed with sadness: "Are ruins, then, already here?"

LIFE IN THE WILDERNESS [2]

From time to time we come to fresh clearings; all these places are alike; I shall describe the one at which we halted tonight, since it will serve me for a picture of all the others.

The bell which the pioneers hang round the necks of their cattle, in order to find them again in the woods, announced from afar our approach to a clearing; and we soon afterwards heard the stroke of the axe, hewing down the trees of the forest. As we came nearer, traces of destruction marked the presence of civilized man: the road was strewn with cut boughs; trunks of trees, half consumed by fire, or mutilated by the axe, were still standing in our way. We proceeded till we reached a wood in which all the trees seemed to have been suddenly struck dead; in the middle of summer their boughs were as leafless as in winter; and upon closer examination we found that a deep circle had been cut through the bark, which, by stopping the circulation of the sap, soon kills the tree. We were informed that this is commonly the first thing a pioneer does, as he cannot, in the first year, cut down all the trees that cover his new domain; he sows Indian corn under their branches, and puts the trees to death in order to prevent them from injuring his crop.

[2] Text from *Democracy in America*, by Alexis de Tocqueville (1805–1859), French writer, political philosopher, and government official. Knopf. '45. 2v. v 2, p 362–5. Copyright © 1945, renewed 1973, by Alfred A. Knopf, Inc. Reprinted by permission of the publisher.

Beyond this field, at present imperfectly traced out, the first work of civilization in the desert, we suddenly came upon the cabin of its owner, situated in the center of a plot of ground more carefully cultivated than the rest, but where man was still waging unequal warfare with the forest; there the trees were cut down, but not uprooted, and the trunks still encumbered the ground which they so recently shaded. Around these dry blocks, wheat, oak seedlings, and plants of every kind grow and intertwine in all the luxuriance of wild, untutored nature. Amid this vigorous and varied vegetation stands the house of the pioneer, or, as they call it, the *log house*. Like the ground about it, this rustic dwelling bore marks of recent and hasty labor: its length seemed not to exceed thirty feet, its height fifteen; the walls as well as the roof were formed of rough trunks of trees, between which a little moss and clay had been inserted to keep out the cold and rain.

As night was coming on, we determined to ask the master of the log house for a lodging. At the sound of our footsteps the children who were playing among the scattered branches sprang up, and ran towards the house, as if they were frightened at the sight of man; while two large dogs, half wild, with ears erect and outstretched nose, came growling out of their hut to cover the retreat of their young masters. The pioneer himself appeared at the door of his dwelling; he looked at us with a rapid and inquisitive glance, made a sign to the dogs to go into the house, and set them the example, without betraying either curiosity or apprehension at our arrival.

We entered the log house: the inside is quite unlike that of the cottages of the peasantry of Europe; it contains more that is superfluous, less that is necessary. A single window with a muslin curtain; on a hearth of trodden clay an immense fire, which lights the whole interior; above the hearth, a good rifle, a deerskin, and plumes of eagles' feathers; on the right hand of the chimney, a map of the

United States, raised and shaken by the wind through the crannies in the wall; near the map, on a shelf formed of a roughly hewn plank, a few volumes of books: a Bible, the first six books of Milton, and two of Shakespeare's plays; along the wall, trunks instead of closets; in the center of the room, a rude table, with legs of green wood with the bark still on them, looking as if they grew out of the ground on which they stood; but on this table a teapot of British china, silver spoons, cracked teacups, and some newspapers.

The master of this dwelling has the angular features and lank limbs peculiar to the native of New England. It is evident that this man was not born in the solitude in which we have found him: his physical constitution suffices to show that his earlier years were spent in the midst of civilized society and that he belongs to that restless, calculating, and adventurous race of men who do with the utmost coolness things only to be accounted for by the ardor of passion, and who endure the life of savages for a time in order to conquer and civilize the backwoods.

When the pioneer perceived that we were crossing his threshold, he came to meet us and shake hands, as is their custom; but his face was quite unmoved. He opened the conversation by inquiring what was going on in the world; and when his curiosity was satisfied, he held his peace, as if he were tired of the noise and importunity of mankind. When we questioned him in our turn, he gave us all the information we asked; he then attended sedulously, but without eagerness, to our wants. While he was engaged in providing thus kindly for us, how did it happen that, in spite of ourselves, we felt our gratitude die on our lips? It is that our host, while he performs the duties of hospitality, seems to be obeying a painful obligation of his station; he treats it as a duty imposed upon him by his situation, not as a pleasure.

By the side of the hearth sits a woman with a baby on her lap; she nods to us without disturbing herself. Like the pioneer, this woman is in the prime of life; her appearance seems superior to her condition, and her apparel even betrays a lingering taste for dress; but her delicate limbs appear shrunken, her features are drawn in, her eye is mild and melancholy; her whole physiognomy bears marks of religious resignation, a deep quiet of all passions, and some sort of natural and tranquil firmness, ready to meet all the ills of life without fearing and without braving them.

Her children cluster about her, full of health, turbulence, and energy: they are true children of the wilderness. Their mother watches them from time to time with mingled melancholy and joy: to look at their strength and her languor, one might imagine that the life she has given them has exhausted her own, and still she does not regret what they have cost her.

The house inhabited by these emigrants has no internal partition or loft. In the one chamber of which it consists the whole family is gathered for the night. The dwelling is itself a little world, an ark of civilization amid an ocean of foliage: a hundred steps beyond it the primeval forest spreads its shades, and solitude resumes its sway.

EXPERIMENT IN HOMESTEADING [3]

When I wrote the following pages, or rather the bulk of them, I lived alone, in the woods, a mile from any neighbor, in a house which I had built myself, on the shore of Walden Pond, in Concord, Massachusetts, and earned my living by the labor of my hands only. I lived there two years and two months. At present I am a sojourner in civilized life again. . . .

Near the end of March, 1845, I borrowed an axe and went down to the woods by Walden Pond, nearest to where I intended to build my house, and began to cut down some

[3] Excerpts from *Walden and Other Writings of Henry David Thoreau*. Text from Modern Library College Editions. Random House. '50. p 3, 36–63.

tall arrowy white pines, still in their youth, for timber. It is difficult to begin without borrowing, but perhaps it is the most generous course thus to permit your fellow-men to have an interest in your enterprise. The owner of the axe, as he released his hold on it, said that it was the apple of his eye; but I returned it sharper than I received it. It was a pleasant hillside where I worked, covered with pine woods, through which I looked out on the pond, and a small open field in the woods where pines and hickories were springing up. The ice in the pond was not yet dissolved, though there were some open spaces, and it was all dark colored and saturated with water. There were some slight flurries of snow during the days that I worked there; but for the most part when I came out on to the railroad, on my way home, its yellow sand heap stretched away gleaming in the hazy atmosphere, and the rails shone in the spring sun, and I heard the lark and pewee and other birds already come to commence another year with us. They were pleasant spring days, in which the winter of man's discontent was thawing as well as the earth, and the life that had lain torpid began to stretch itself. One day, when my axe had come off and I had cut a green hickory for a wedge, driving it with a stone, and had placed the whole to soak in a pond hole in order to swell the wood, I saw a striped snake run into the water, and he lay on the bottom, apparently without inconvenience, as long as I stayed there, or more than a quarter of an hour; perhaps because he had not yet fairly come out of the torpid state. It appeared to me that for a like reason men remain in their present low and primitive condition; but if they should feel the influence of the spring of springs arousing them, they would of necessity rise to a higher and more ethereal life. I had previously seen the snakes in frosty mornings in my path with portions of their bodies still numb and inflexible, waiting for the sun to thaw them. On the 1st of April it rained and melted the ice, and in the early part of the day, which was very foggy, I heard a stray goose groping about over the pond and cackling as if lost, or like the spirit of the fog.

So I went on for some days cutting and hewing timber, and also studs and rafters, all with my narrow axe, not having many communicable or scholar-like thoughts, singing to myself,—

> Men say they know many things;
> But lo! they have taken wings,—
> The arts and sciences,
> And a thousand appliances;
> The wind that blows
> Is all that anybody knows.

I hewed the main timbers six inches square, most of the studs on two sides only, and the rafters and floor timbers on one side, leaving the rest of the bark on, so that they were just as straight and much stronger than sawed ones. Each stick was carefully mortised or tenoned by its stump, for I had borrowed other tools by this time. My days in the woods were not very long ones; yet I usually carried my dinner of bread and butter, and read the newspaper in which it was wrapped, at noon, sitting amid the green pine boughs which I had cut off, and to my bread was imparted some of their fragrance, for my hands were covered with a thick coat of pitch. Before I had done I was more the friend than the foe of the pine tree, though I had cut down some of them, having become better acquainted with it. Sometimes a rambler in the woods was attracted by the sound of my axe, and we chatted pleasantly over the chips which I had made. . . .

I dug my cellar in the side of a hill sloping to the south, where a woodchuck had formerly dug his burrow, down through sumach and blackberry roots, and the lowest stain of vegetation, six feet square by seven deep, to a fine sand where potatoes would not freeze in any winter. The sides were left shelving, and not stoned; but the sun having never shone on them, the sand still keeps its place. It was but two hours' work. I took particular pleasure in this breaking of ground, for in almost all latitudes men dig into the earth for an equable temperature. Under the most splendid house in the city is still to be found the cellar where they store their roots as of old, and long after the superstructure has disappeared posterity remark its dent in the earth. The house is still but a sort of porch at the entrance of a burrow.

At length, in the beginning of May, with the help of some of my acquaintances, rather to improve so good an occasion for neighborliness than from any necessity, I set up the frame of my house. No man was ever more honored in the character of his raisers than I. They are destined, I trust, to assist at the raising of loftier structures one day. I began to occupy my house on the 4th of July, as soon as it was boarded and roofed, for the boards were carefully feather-edged and lapped, so that it was perfectly impervious to rain; but before boarding I laid the foundation of a chimney at one end, bringing two cartloads of stones up the hill from the pond in my arms. I built the chimney after my hoeing in the fall, before a fire became necessary for warmth, doing my cooking in the meanwhile out of doors on the ground, early in the morning: which mode I still think is in some respects more convenient and agreeable than the usual one. When it stormed before my bread was baked, I fixed a few boards over the fire, and sat under them to watch my loaf, and passed some pleasant hours in that way. In those days, when my hands were much employed, I read but little, but the least scraps of paper which lay on the ground, my holder, or tablecloth, afforded me as much entertainment, in fact answered the same purpose as the Iliad.

It would be worth the while to build still more deliberately than I did, considering, for instance, what foundation, a door, a window, a cellar, a garret, have in the nature of man, and perchance never raising any superstructure until we found a better reason for it than our temporal necessities, even. . . .

Before winter I built a chimney, and shingled the sides of my house, which were already impervious to rain, with imperfect and sappy shingles made of the first slice of the log, whose edges I was obliged to straighten with a plane.

I have thus a tight shingled and plastered house, ten feet wide by fifteen long, and eight-feet posts, with a garret and a closet, a large window on each side, two trap doors, one door at the end, and a brick fireplace opposite. The exact cost of my house, paying the usual price for such materials as I used, but not counting the work, all of which was done by myself, was as follows; and I give the details because very few are able to tell exactly what their houses cost, and fewer still, if any, the separate cost of the various materials which compose them:—

Boards,	$8 03½,	mostly shanty boards.
Refuse shingles for roof and sides,	4 00	
Laths,	1 25	
Two second-hand windows with glass,	2 43	
One thousand old brick,	4 00	
Two casks of lime,	2 40	That was high.
Hair,	0 31	More than I needed.
Mantle-tree iron,	0 15	
Nails,	3 90	
Hinges and screws,	0 14	
Latch,	0 10	
Chalk,	0 01	
Transportation,	1 40	} I carried a good part on my back.
In all,	$28 12½	

These are all the materials excepting the timber stones and sand, which I claimed by squatter's right. I have also a small wood-shed adjoining, made chiefly of the stuff which was left after building the house. . . . .

Before I finished my house, wishing to earn ten or twelve dollars by some honest and agreeable method, in order to meet my unusual expenses, I planted about two acres and a half of light and sandy soil near it chiefly with beans, but also a small part with potatoes, corn, peas, and turnips. The whole lot contains eleven acres, mostly growing up to pines and hickories, and was sold the preceding season for eight dollars and eight cents an acre. One farmer said that it was "good for nothing but to raise cheeping squirrels on." I put no manure on this land, not being the owner, but merely a squatter, and not expecting to cultivate so much again, and I did not quite hoe it all once. I got out several cords of stumps in ploughing, which supplied me with fuel for a long time, and left small circles of virgin mould, easily distinguishable through the summer by the greater luxuriance of the beans there. The dead and for the most part unmerchantable wood behind my house, and the driftwood from the pond, have supplied the remainder of my fuel. I was obliged to hire a team and a man for the ploughing, though I held the plough myself. My farm outgoes for the first season were, for implements, seed, work, &c., $14 72½. The seed corn was given me. This never costs anything to speak of, unless you plant more than enough. I got twelve bushels of beans, and eighteen bushels of potatoes, beside some peas and sweet corn. The yellow corn and turnips were too late to come to anything. My whole income from the farm was

	$23 44.
Deducting the outgoes, ...	14 72½
there are left, ...	$ 8 71½,

beside produce consumed and on hand at the time this estimate was made of the value of $4 50,—the amount on hand much more than balancing a little grass which I did not raise. All things considered, that is, considering the importance of a man's soul and of to-day, notwithstanding the short time occupied by my experiment, nay, partly even because of its transient character, I believe that that was doing better than any farmer in Concord did that year.

The next year I did better still, for I spaded up all the land which I required, about a third of an acre, and I learned from the experience of both years, not being in the least awed by many celebrated works on husbandry, Arthur Young among the rest, that if one would live simply and eat only the crop which he raised, and raise no more than he ate, and not exchange it for an insufficient quantity of more luxurious and expensive things, he would need to cultivate only a few rods of ground, and that it would be cheaper to spade up that than to use oxen to plough it, and to select a fresh spot from time to time than to manure the old, and he could do all his necessary farm work as it were with his left hand at odd hours in the summer; and thus he would not be tied to an ox, or horse, or cow, or pig, as at present. I desire to speak impartially on this point, and as one not interested in the success or failure of the present economical and social arrangements. I was more independent than any farmer in Concord, for I was not anchored to a house or farm, but could follow the bent of my genius, which is a very crooked one, every moment. Beside being better off than they already, if my house had been burned or my crops had failed, I should have been nearly as well off as before. . . .

By surveying, carpentry, and day-labor of various other kinds in the village in the meanwhile, for I have as many trades as fingers, I had earned $13 34. The expense of food for eight months, namely, from July 4th to March 1st, the time when these estimates were made, though I lived there more than two years,—not counting potatoes, a little green corn, and some peas, which I had raised, nor considering the value of what was on hand at the last date, was

Rice,	$1 73½	
Molasses,	1 73	Cheapest form of the saccharine.
Rye meal,	1 04¾	
Indian meal,	0 99¾	Cheaper than rye.
Pork,	0 22	
Flour,	0 88	} Costs more than Indian meal, both money and trouble.
Sugar,	0 80	
Lard,	0 65	
Apples,	0 25	
Dried apple,	0 22	
Sweet potatoes,	0 10	
One pumpkin,	0 6	
One watermelon,	0 2	
Salt,	0 3	

All experiments which failed.

Yes, I did eat $8 74, all told; but I should not thus un-blushingly publish my guilt, if I did not know that most of my readers were equally guilty with myself, and that their deeds would look no better in print. The next year I some-times caught a mess of fish for my dinner, and once I went so far as to slaughter a woodchuck which ravaged my bean-field,—effect his transmigration, as a Tartar would say,—and devour him, partly for experiment's sake; but though it afforded me a momentary enjoyment, notwithstanding a musky flavor, I saw that the longest use would not make that a good practice, however it might seem to have your woodchucks ready dressed by the village butcher.

Clothing and some incidental expenses within the same dates, though little can be inferred from this item, amounted to

$8 40¾

Oil and some household utensils, ... 2 00

So that all the pecuniary outgoes, excepting for washing and mending, which for the most part were done out of the house, and their bills have not yet been received,—and these are all and more than all the ways by which money neces-sarily goes out in this part of the world,—were

House,	$28 12½
Farm one year,	14 72½
Food eight months,	8 74
Clothing, &c., eight months,	8 40¾
Oil, &c., eight months,	2 00
In all,	$61 99¾

I address myself now to those of my readers who have a living to get. And to meet this I have for farm produce sold

	$23 44
Earned by day-labor,	13 34
In all,	$36 78,

which subtracted from the sum of the outgoes leaves a balance of $25 21¾ on the one side,—this being very nearly the means with which I started, and the measure of expenses to be incurred,—and on the other, beside the leisure and independence and health thus secured, a comfortable house for me as long as I choose to occupy it. . . .

For more than five years I maintained myself thus solely by the labor of my hands, and I found, that by working about six weeks in a year, I could meet all the expenses of living. The whole of my winters, as well as most of my summers, I had free and clear for study. I have thoroughly tried school-keeping, and found that my expenses were in proportion, or rather out of proportion, to my income, for I was obliged to dress and train, not to say think and believe, accordingly, and I lost my time into the bargain. As I did not teach for the good of my fellow-men, but simply for a livelihood, this was a failure. I have tried trade; but I found that it would take ten years to get under way in that, and that then I should probably be on my way to the devil. I was actually afraid that I might by that time be doing what is called a good business. When formerly I was looking about to see what I could do for a living, some sad experience in conforming to the wishes of friends being fresh in my mind to tax my ingenuity, I thought often and seriously of picking huckleberries; that surely I could do, and its small profits might suffice,—for my greatest skill has been to want but little,—so little capital it required, so little distraction from my wonted moods, I foolishly thought. While my acquaintances went unhesitatingly into trade or the professions, I contemplated this occupation as most like theirs; ranging the hills all summer to pick the berries which came in my way, and thereafter carelessly dispose of them; so, to keep the flocks of Admetus. I also dreamed that I might gather the wild herbs, or carry evergreens to such villagers as loved to be reminded of the woods, even to the city, by hay-cart loads. But I have since learned that trade curses every thing it handles; and though you trade in messages from heaven, the whole curse of trade attaches to the business.

As I preferred some things to others, and especially valued my freedom, as I could fare hard and yet succeed well, I did not wish to spend my time in earning rich carpets or other fine furniture or delicate cookery, or a house in the Grecian or the Gothic style just yet. If there are any to whom it is no interruption to acquire these things, and who know how to use them when acquired, I relinquish to them the pursuit. Some are "industrious," and appear to love labor for its own sake, or perhaps because it keeps them out of worse mischief; to such I have at present nothing to say. Those who would not know what to do with more leisure than they now enjoy I might advise to work twice as hard as they do,—work till they pay for themselves, and get their free papers. For myself I found that the occupation of a day-laborer was the most independent of any, especially as it required only thirty or forty days in a year to support one. The laborer's day ends with the going down of the sun, and he is then free to devote himself to his chosen pursuit, independent of his labor; but his employer, who speculates from month to month, has no respite from one end of the year to the other.

GROWING UP IN MISSOURI [4]

I can see the farm yet, with perfect clearness. I can see all its belongings, all its details; the family room of the house, with a "trundle" bed in one corner and a spinning wheel in another—a wheel whose rising and falling wail, heard from a distance, was the mournfulest of all sounds to me and made me homesick and low spirited and filled my atmosphere with the wandering spirits of the dead; the vast fireplace, piled high on winter nights with flaming hickory logs from whose ends a sugary sap bubbled out but did not go to waste, for we scraped it off and ate it; the lazy cat spread out on the rough hearthstones; the drowsy dogs braced against the jambs and blinking; my aunt in one chimney corner, knitting; my uncle in the other, smoking his corncob pipe; the slick and carpetless oak floor faintly mirroring the dancing flame tongues and freckled with black indentations where fire coals had popped out and died a leisurely death; half a dozen children romping in the background twilight; "split"-bottomed chairs here and there, some with rockers; a cradle—out of service but waiting with confidence; in the early cold mornings a snuggle of children in shirts and chemises, occupying the hearthstone and procrastinating—they could not bear to leave that comfortable place and go out on the wind-swept floor space between the house and kitchen where the general tin basin stood, and wash.

Along outside of the front fence ran the country road, dusty in the summertime and a good place for snakes—they liked to lie in it and sun themselves; when they were rattlesnakes or puff adders we killed them; when they were black snakes or racers or belonged to the fabled "hoop" breed we fled without shame; when they were "house snakes" or "garters" we carried them home and put them in Aunt

⁴ Excerpts from *Mark Twain's Autobiography.* Harper. '24. v 1 p 102–4, 106–14. Copyright 1924 by Clara Gabrilowitsch; renewed 1952 by Clara Clemens Samassoud. Reprinted by permission of Harper & Row, Publishers, Inc.

Patsy's work basket for a surprise; for she was prejudiced against snakes, and always when she took the basket in her lap and they began to climb out of it, it disordered her mind. She never could seem to get used to them; her opportunities went for nothing. And she was always cold toward bats, too, and could not bear them; and yet I think a bat is as friendly a bird as there is. My mother was Aunt Patsy's sister and had the same wild superstitions. A bat is beautifully soft and silky; I do not know any creature that is pleasanter to the touch or is more grateful for caressings, if offered in the right spirit. I know all about these coleoptera because our great cave, three miles below Hannibal, was multitudinously stocked with them and often I brought them home to amuse my mother with. It was easy to manage if it was a school day because then I had ostensibly been to school and hadn't any bats. She was not a suspicious person but full of trust and confidence; and when I said, "There's something in my coat pocket for you," she would put her hand in. But she always took it out again, herself; I didn't have to tell her. It was remarkable the way she couldn't learn to like private bats. The more experience she had the more she could not change her views. . . .

Beyond the road where the snakes sunned themselves was a dense young thicket and through it a dim-lighted path led a quarter of a mile; then out of the dimness one emerged abruptly upon a level great prairie which was covered with wild strawberry plants, vividly starred with prairie pinks and walled in on all sides by forests. The strawberries were fragrant and fine, and in the season we were generally there in the crisp freshness of the early morning, while the dew beads still sparkled upon the grass and the woods were ringing with the first songs of the birds.

Down the forest slopes to the left were the swings. They were made of bark stripped from hickory saplings. When they became dry they were dangerous. They usually broke when a child was forty feet in the air and this was why so many bones had to be mended every year. I had no ill luck myself but none of my cousins escaped. There were eight of them and at one time and another they broke fourteen arms among them. But it cost next to nothing, for the doctor worked by the year—twenty-five dollars for the whole family. I remember two of the Florida doctors, Chowning and Meredith. They not only tended an entire family for twenty-five dollars a year but furnished the medicines themselves. Good measure, too. Only the largest persons could hold a whole dose. Castor oil was the principal beverage. The dose was half a dipperful, with half a dipperful of New Orleans molasses added to help it down and make it taste good, which it never did. The next standby was calomel; the next rhubarb; and the next jalap. Then they bled the patient and put mustard plasters on him. It was a dreadful system and yet the death rate was not heavy. The calomel was nearly sure to salivate the patient and cost him some of his teeth. There were no dentists. When teeth became touched with decay or were otherwise ailing, the doctor knew of but one thing to do—he fetched his tongs and dragged them out. If the jaw remained, it was not his fault.

Doctors were not called in cases of ordinary illness; the family grandmother attended to those. Every old woman was a doctor and gathered her own medicines in the woods and knew how to compound doses that would stir the vitals of a cast-iron dog. And then there was the "Indian doctor"; a grave savage, remnant of his tribe, deeply read in the mysteries of nature and the secret properties of herbs; and most backwoodsmen had high faith in his powers and could tell of wonderful cures achieved by him. In Mauritius, away off yonder in the solitudes of the Indian Ocean, there is a person who answers to our Indian doctor of the old times. He is a Negro and has had no teaching as a doctor, yet there is one disease which he is master of and can cure and the doctors can't. They send for him when they have a case. It is a child's disease of a strange and deadly sort and the Negro cures it with a herb medicine which he makes himself from a prescription which has come down to him from his father and grandfather. He will not let anyone see it. He keeps the secret of its components to himself and it is feared that he will die without divulging it; then there will be consternation in Mauritius. I was told these things by the people there in 1896.

We had the "faith doctor," too, in those early days—a woman. Her specialty was toothache. She was a farmer's old wife and lived five miles from Hannibal. She would lay her hand on the patient's jaw and say, "Believe!" and the cure was prompt. Mrs. Utterback. I remember her very well. Twice I rode out there behind my mother, horseback, and saw the cure performed. My mother was the patient.

Doctor Meredith removed to Hannibal by and by and was our family physician there and saved my life several times. Still, he was a good man and meant well. Let it go.

I was always told that I was a sickly and precarious and tiresome and uncertain child and lived mainly on allopathic medicines during the first seven years of my life. I asked my mother about this, in her old age—she was in her eighty-eighth year—and said:

"I suppose that during all that time you were uneasy about me?"

"Yes, the whole time."

"Afraid I wouldn't live?"

After a reflective pause—ostensibly to think out the facts —"No—afraid you would."

It sounds like plagiarism but it probably wasn't.

The country schoolhouse was three miles from my uncle's farm. It stood in a clearing in the woods and would hold about twenty-five boys and girls. We attended the school with more or less regularity once or twice a week, in summer, walking to it in the cool of the morning by the forest paths and back in the gloaming at the end of the day. All the pupils brought their dinners in baskets—corn dodger, buttermilk and other good things—and sat in the shade of the trees at noon and ate them. It is the part of my education which I look back upon with the most satisfaction. My first visit to the school was when I was seven. A strapping girl of fifteen, in the customary sunbonnet and calico dress, asked me if I "used tobacco"—meaning did I chew it. I said no. It roused her scorn. She reported me to all the crowd and said:

"Here is a boy seven years old who can't chaw tobacco."

By the looks and comments which this produced I realized that I was a degraded object; I was cruelly ashamed of myself. I determined to reform. But I only made myself sick; I was not able to learn to chew tobacco. I learned to smoke fairly well but that did not conciliate anybody and I remained a poor thing and characterless. I longed to be respected but I never was able to rise. Children have but little charity for one another's defects.

As I have said, I spent some part of every year at the farm until I was twelve or thirteen years old. The life which I led there with my cousins was full of charm, and so is the memory of it yet. I can call back the solemn twilight and mystery of the deep woods, the earthy smells, the faint odors of the wild flowers, the sheen of rain-washed foliage, the rattling clatter of drops when the wind shook the trees, the far-off hammering of woodpeckers and the muffled drumming of wood pheasants in the remoteness of the forest, the snapshot glimpses of disturbed wild creatures scurrying through the grass—I can call it all back and make it as real as it ever was, and as blessed. I can call back the prairie, and its loneliness and peace, and a vast hawk hanging motionless in the sky, with his wings spread wide and the blue of the vault showing through the fringe of their end feathers. I can see the woods in their autumn dress, the oaks purple, the hickories washed with gold, the maples and the sumachs luminous with crimson fires, and I can hear the rustle made by the fallen leaves as we plowed through them. I can see the blue clusters of wild grapes hanging among the foliage of the saplings, and I remember the taste of them and the smell. I know how the wild blackberries looked, and how they tasted, and the same with the paw-

paws, the hazelnuts, and the persimmons; and I can feel the thumping rain, upon my head, of hickory nuts and walnuts when we were out in the frosty dawn to scramble for them with the pigs, and the gusts of wind loosed them and sent them down. I know the stain of blackberries, and how pretty it is, and I know the stain of walnut hulls, and how little it minds soap and water, also what grudged experience it had of either of them. I know the taste of maple sap, and when to gather it, and how to arrange the troughs and the delivery tubes, and how to boil down the juice, and how to hook the sugar after it is made, also how much better hooked sugar tastes than any that is honestly come by, let bigots say what they will. I know how a prize watermelon looks when it is sunning its fat rotundity among pumpkin vines and "simblins"; I know how to tell when it is ripe without "plugging" it; I know how inviting it looks when it is cooling itself in a tub of water under the bed, waiting; I know how it looks when it lies on the table in the sheltered great floor space between house and kitchen, and the children gathered for the sacrifice and their mouths watering; I know the crackling sound it makes when the carving knife enters its end, and I can see the split fly along in front of the blade as the knife cleaves its way to the other end; I can see its halves fall apart and display the rich red meat and the black seeds, and the heart standing up, a luxury fit for the elect; I know how a boy looks behind a yard-long slice of that melon, and I know how he feels; for I have been there. I know the taste of the watermelon which has been honestly come by, and I know the taste of the watermelon which has been acquired by art. Both taste good, but the experienced know which tastes best. I know the look of green apples and peaches and pears on the trees, and I know how entertaining they are when they are inside of a person. I know how ripe ones look when they are piled in pyramids under the trees, and how pretty they are and how vivid their colors. I know how a frozen apple looks, in a barrel down cellar in the wintertime, and how hard it is to bite, and how the frost

makes the teeth ache, and yet how good it is, notwithstanding. I know the disposition of elderly people to select the
speckled apples for the children, and I once knew ways to
beat the game. I know the look of an apple that is roasting
and sizzling on a hearth on a winter's evening, and I know
the comfort that comes of eating it hot, along with some
sugar and a drench of cream. I know the delicate art and
mystery of so cracking hickory nuts and walnuts on a flat-
iron with a hammer that the kernels will be delivered
whole, and I know how the nuts, taken in conjunction with
winter apples, cider, and doughnuts, make old people's old
tales and old jokes sound fresh and crisp and enchanting,
and juggle an evening away before you know what went
with the time. I know the look of Uncle Dan'l's kitchen as
it was on the privileged nights, when I was a child, and I
can see the white and black children grouped on the hearth,
with the firelight playing on their faces and the shadows
flickering upon the walls, clear back toward the cavernous
gloom of the rear, and I can hear Uncle Dan'l telling the
immortal tales which Uncle Remus Harris was to gather
into his books and charm the world with, by and by; and
I can feel again the creepy joy which quivered through me
when the time for the ghost story of the "Golden Arm" was
reached—and the sense of regret, too, which came over me,
for it was always the last story of the evening and there was
nothing between it and the unwelcome bed.

I can remember the bare wooden stairway in my uncle's
house, and the turn to the left above the landing, and the
rafters and the slanting roof over my bed, and the squares
of moonlight on the floor, and the white cold world of snow
outside, seen through the curtainless window. I can remember
the howling of the wind and the quaking of the house on
stormy nights, and how snug and cozy one felt, under the
blankets, listening; and how the powdery snow used to sift
in, around the sashes, and lie in little ridges on the floor and
make the place look chilly in the morning and curb the
wild desire to get up—in case there was any. I can remember

how very dark that room was, in the dark of the moon, and
how packed it was with ghostly stillness when one woke up
by accident away in the night, and forgotten sins came flock-
ing out of the secret chambers of the memory and wanted a
hearing; and how ill chosen the time seemed for this kind
of business; and how dismal was the hoo-hooing of the owl
and the wailing of the wolf, sent mourning by on the night
wind.

I remember the raging of the rain on that roof, summer
nights, and how pleasant it was to lie and listen to it, and
enjoy the white splendor of the lightning and the majestic
booming and crashing of the thunder. It was a very satisfactory room, and there was a lightning rod which was reach-
able from the window, an adorable and skittish thing to
climb up and down, summer nights, when there were duties
on hand of a sort to make privacy desirable.

I remember the 'coon and 'possum hunts, nights, with
the Negroes, and the long marches through the black gloom
of the woods, and the excitement which fired everybody
when the distant bay of an experienced dog announced
that the game was treed; then the wild scramblings and
stumblings through briers and bushes and over roots to get
to the spot; then the lighting of a fire and the felling of the
tree, the joyful frenzy of the dogs and the Negroes, and the
weird picture it all made in the red glare—I remember it all
well, and the delight that everyone got out of it, except the
'coon.

I remember the pigeon seasons, when the birds would
come in millions and cover the trees and by their weight
break down the branches. They were clubbed to death with
sticks; guns were not necessary and were not used. I remember the squirrel hunts, and prairie-chicken hunts, and wild-
turkey hunts, and all that; and how we turned out, mornings, while it was still dark, to go on these expeditions, and
how chilly and dismal it was, and how often I regretted
that I was well enough to go. A toot on a tin horn brought
twice as many dogs as were needed, and in their happiness

they raced and scampered about, and knocked small people down, and made no end of unnecessary noise. At the word, they vanished away toward the woods, and we drifted silently after them in the melancholy gloom. But presently the gray dawn stole over the world, the birds piped up, then the sun rose and poured light and comfort all around, everything was fresh and dewy and fragrant, and life was a boon again. After three hours of tramping we arrived back wholesomely tired, overladen with game, very hungry, and just in time for breakfast. . . .

MISSISSIPPI RIVER PILOTS [5]

I remember the Mississippi River. I used to be drowned in it regularly, every summer, and then be fished out and drained out and inflated and set going again by some chance enemy of the human race. But it never seemed to bother my mother; she would only smile and say, "People born to be hanged are safe in water."

When I was a boy, there was but one permanent ambition among my comrades in our village [Hannibal, Missouri] on the west bank of the Mississippi River. That was, to be a steamboatman. We had transient ambitions of other sorts, but they were only transient. When a circus came and went, it left us all burning to become clowns; the first Negro minstrel show that ever came to our section left us all suffering to try that kind of life; now and then we had a hope that if we lived and were good, God would permit us to be pirates. These ambitions faded out, each in its turn; but the ambition to be a steamboatman always remained.

Boy after boy managed to get on the river. By and by, I ran away. I said I would never come home again till I was a pilot and could come in glory.

I became apprenticed to Mr. Bixby of the *Paul Jones*. He

[5] Excerpts from *Life on the Mississippi* by Mark Twain. Text from Dodd, Mead edition. [1968?] p 29, 32–3, 54, 317–18.

agreed to teach me the Mississippi River from New Orleans to St. Louis for five hundred dollars, payable out of the first wages I should receive after graduating. I entered upon the small enterprise of "learning" twelve or thirteen hundred miles of the great Mississippi River with the easy confidence of my time of life. If I had really known what I was about to require of my faculties, I should not have had the courage to begin. I supposed that all a pilot had to do was to keep his boat in the river and I did not consider that that could be much of a trick, since it was so wide.

One cannot easily realize what a tremendous thing it is to know every trivial detail of twelve hundred miles of river and know it with absolute exactness. If you take the longest street in New York, and travel up and down it, conning its features patiently until you know every house and window and lamp post and big and little signs by heart, and know them so accurately that you can instantly name the one you are abreast of when you are set down at random in that street in the middle of an inky black night, you will then have a tolerable notion of the amount and the exactness of a pilot's knowledge who carries the Mississippi River in his head. And then, if you will go on until you know every street-crossing, the character, size, and position of the crossing-stones, and the varying depths of mud in each of these numberless places, you will have some idea of what the pilot must know in order to keep the Mississippi steamer out of trouble. Next, if you will take half of the signs in that long street, and *change their places* once a month, and still manage to know their new positions accurately on dark nights, and keep up with these repeated changes without making any mistakes, you will understand what is required of a pilot's peerless memory by the fickle Mississippi. . . .

The Pilot-Farmer

In the course of the tugboat gossip, it came out that out of every five of my former friends who had quitted the river, four had chosen farming as an occupation. Of course this was not because they were peculiarly gifted agriculturally, and thus more likely to succeed as farmers than in other industries: the reason for their choice must be traced to some other source. Doubtless they chose farming because that life is private and secluded from irruptions of undesirable strangers—like the pilot-house hermitage. And doubtless they also chose it because on a thousand nights of black storm and danger they had noted the twinkling lights of solitary farmhouses, as the boat swung by and pictured to themselves the serenity and security and coziness of such refuge, at such times, and so had by and by come to dream of that retired and peaceful life as the one desirable thing to long for, anticipate, earn, and at last enjoy.

But I did not learn that any of these pilot farmers had astonished anybody with their success. Their farms do not support them: they support their farms. The pilot-farmer disappears from the river annually, about the breaking of spring, and is seen no more till next frost. Then he appears again, in damaged homespun, combs the hayseed out of his hair, and takes a pilot-house berth for the winter. In this way he pays the debts which his farming has achieved during the agricultural season. So his river bondage is but half broken; he is still the river's slave the hardest half of the year.

One of these men bought a farm, but did not retire to it. He knew a trick worth two of that. He did not propose to pauperize his farm by applying his personal ignorance to working it. No, he put the farm into the hands of an agricultural expert to be worked on shares—out of every three loads of corn the expert to have two and the pilot the third. But at the end of the season the pilot received no corn. The expert explained that *his* share was not reached. The farm produced only two loads.

PEDDLERS [6]

By the beginning of the eighteenth century, the New England peddler was traveling all over the West and South. Peddling was already recognized as a way to wealth, and sons of peddlers were rising into the merchant class. Richardson Wright, author of one of the best books about this period [*Hawkers & Walkers in Early America*], cites a visitor to Boston in 1699 who observed that "in the chief of High Street there are stately edifices, some of which cost the owners two or three thousand pounds the raising . . . for the fathers of these men were tinkers and peddlers."

In 1740, the arrival in Berlin, Connecticut, of two Irish tinsmiths started the transformation of the random wandering of the Yankee peddlers into something resembling a sales force for American industry, then in its infant years.

A great tinware boom was set off by Edgar and William Pattison, who emigrated from County Tyrone in 1738.

The colonial household was not a place of great adornment. Purchases were few and limited to necessities, though many a farmer's wife must have longed for a bit of finery. The silver-bright gleam of tin pots and pans tapped the unsuspected reservoirs of pent-up colonial consumer demand. Most housewives were eager to have this gleaming replacement for their dull and dented pewter, although it was not popular at the higher levels of society. When a tavern-keeper set George Washington's table with tin utensils, the General sent a boy over to the home of a local judge to borrow some silverware for the meal. Fortunately for tin peddlers, Virginia aristocrats did not comprise a large part of the potential market.

Tinware was no innovation. Indian traders had swapped tin dishes for furs as early as 1584. Its subsequent absence from the American table ended when the Pattisons, by ac-

[6] From *The Traveling Man* by Truman E. Moore, free-lance writer. Doubleday. '72. p 4–20. Copyright © 1972 by Truman E. Moore. Used by permission of Doubleday & Company, Inc.

cident or design, discovered the market. The traveling salesman has often been called a civilizing influence because he
carried the latest products and newest inventions to the far
reaches of the world. The benefits to civilization from tinware may not have been great, but in the hands of the
peddlers, tinware appeared on the tables of the remotest
cabin, and no trail was left untrod.

The Pattisons' shop in Berlin, Connecticut, produced
various tin items—plates, cups, spoons, forks, pans, pitchers,
and pails. They peddled their stock around town and then
retired to the shop to make more. The business prospered
and they found it necessary to hire apprentices and peddlers
to cover Connecticut and the surrounding colonies. Tin
peddlers were soon making regular trips into the South and
West. Other tinware shops opened, and for the next hundred years Berlin was the center of the tinware business.
After its decline, the region remained a center for the metal
and hardware industry, as it is today.

The growth of peddling as a business encountered one
serious difficulty. By the nineteenth century, most states had
laws either licensing or restricting peddlers.

The storekeepers, many of whom were themselves former
peddlers, watched the passing parade of Yankee peddlers
with growing resentment. Feeling that their domain was
being invaded, the local merchants began to assert their
territorial imperative by bringing pressure on the legisla-
ture for laws against peddling. A series of fines and restrictions against peddlers in Rhode Island finally culminated
in 1728 in an outright ban on peddling. Pennsylvania began
to license peddlers, and Connecticut—the great source of
most of the commercial wanderers—placed a heavy tax on
goods brought into the state. Connecticut merchants peti-
tioned the government to ban all peddlers from entry because "they carried contagious diseases." Presumably, Connecticut peddlers were immune to infection.

Years later, after time and progress had made the peddler obsolete, the laws remained on the books, and the feel-

ing against the intrusion of outsiders remained unshaken. Traveling salesmen on the road before the Civil War were fined and jailed with the old peddler laws or with new laws against salesmen who carried samples. On the outskirts of many small towns today are signs declaring "No peddling or soliciting," though the ordinance is often unenforced.

The trickle of peddlers that annoyed merchants and storekeepers grew to a steadier stream each year despite prohibitive laws. It was perhaps his uncertain standing with the law and his popularity with his customers that gave the peddler an ambivalent status borne by salesmen ever since.

In order to circumvent the antipeddler laws, which proliferated along the Eastern Seaboard, the tinsmiths set up shops and warehouses in the southern and midwestern states. In so doing, the peddler could rightfully claim that his product was of local manufacture and gain immunity from legal harassment. Later, the clock peddlers used the same procedure, setting up assembly shops in the South, where clocks were simply put together and adjusted. It pleased local residents to think that such complicated mechanisms were being made in their own state.

The supply routes thus established—with warehouses and distribution points—became the framework for the wholesale and retail trade of today.

The number of peddlers on the road grew constantly. In good times the stories of success told by returning peddlers attracted others to take up the pack. In bad times the lack of opportunity at home forced many young men to try their hand at peddling.

During the Revolution there was the usual amount of wartime profiteering by wholesalers, big merchants, little storekeepers, and Yankee peddlers. Unfortunately, the peddler was made the most frequent object of the patriot's outrage. [According to J. T. Adams's *New England in the Republic*] complaints were heard that peddlers and "persons no one ever heard of" had "risen to affluence and were usurping the places of the old families." Upward mobility was not yet appreciated, as we can clearly see by the reactions of an officer of the Continental Army who encountered four travelers on the road, all wearing uniforms resplendent with swords and cockades. They stopped at an inn, where six other similarly dressed fellows joined them. The officer supposed them to be soldiers and was shocked to learn that they were "itinerant traders" who boasted of the fabulous sums they made selling and trading from town to town.

Returning home to his own farm, the officer discovered that his hired man had quit to become a peddler, and no amount of pleading or threatening could get him back. The former hired man offered instead to buy his master's Army coat, complaining that he lacked a proper one befitting his new occupation. The indignant officer retired to the Golden Ball Tavern—by the fireside, I imagine, and with a mug of rum flip at his elbow—and penned a letter to the editor of the Hartford *Courant*, and thus left his observations and his outrage to history. . . .

The number of peddlers on the road by the end of the Revolution had fallen to a handful, but after the war ended there were more peddlers than ever. Before 1776, most colonists stayed at home and lived quiet, uneventful lives. Now these men who had marched about in the war saw the peddler's life on the road in a new light. Restless young men who were unwilling to go back to the simple life on the farm, filled a peddler's pack and set out to make a fortune. Some did. Most had a few vagabond years before finding a place to settle down, wiser, and perhaps richer, for the experience.

The Yankee tin peddler became a familiar sight all over the country. The peddler carried his tinware in two trunks slung over his shoulder as he started down the trail. Staggering under the weight of a hundred pounds of tinware and notions, faced with the prospect of marches longer and more burdened than any he ever made in the Army, the young peddler must have recalled his old place at the plow or the apprentice's bench with fond nostalgia and some regret.

After the Revolution, manufactured goods from abroad were again plentiful, and this abundance was added to by the growing industries of New England. There was, however, a shortage of money following the disgrace of the Continental dollar. Prices dropped sharply. . . .

Economic stability had returned by 1790, and the peddlers' prosperity was supplemented unexpectedly by Jefferson's embargo of American ports in an effort to stay out of further trouble with England. . . .

Unpopular with the New England shipping interests and the rural South, the embargo nurtured the growth of domestic industry, much of which relied heavily, and some exclusively, on the peddler for distribution, sales, and advertising. Even after the Revolution, Americans still preferred British goods, and Yankee manufacturers were forced to sell through peddlers.

Unexpected aid for the peddlers came as the result of a prize piece of British folly. At the end of the War of 1812, English manufacturers, alarmed at the persistent growth of American industry, decided to simply put it out of business. Their plan was to undersell American industry to death. American wholesalers watched shiploads of British goods dumped onto the American market at prices representing only a small fraction of their true worth. The American importers went on one of the greatest bargain sprees in history. . . .

For almost a year, British industry flooded American markets with underpriced goods. Peddlers in the port cities crammed their packs with fine goods and headed for the back country. 1815 was the year of the Great Peddler Windfall, and American industry may thank the peddler for his energy. By the end of the year, the English felt the American market was a bottomless pit, and they ceased their expensive methods of trying to fill it.

Industries sprouted all over New England, and there was more for the peddler to sell now than tinware and odds and ends.

Between 1808 and 1815, helped by the extreme protection of Mr. Jefferson's Dambargo [Embargo Act of 1807], and the British blockades before and during the War of 1812, the brass and hardware industries, clock factories, mills, and plants of every sort sprang up beside the streams of the Naugatuck Valley, of which Waterbury was the center. Elsewhere in New England the growth was as rapid. Eli Whitney introduced the factory system by the use of interchangeable parts, and did for manufacturing what his cotton gin had done for agriculture. It is doubtful that any other man had more impact upon American industry than did this Yankee genius.

At first, the pack peddler had brought only the small luxuries and necessities to the cabin door. The tin peddler added more things to his pack, and he prospered and got a horse. The demand for goods and supplies grew with the country. The river towns couldn't get large quantities of supplies to the inland settlements without roads, and the peddler could only carry so much on his back or in his saddlebags. From both the peddlers and the settlers the cry went up for roads, and between 1790 and 1840, America began road-building on a scale not equaled until recent times.

Many of the roads built during this era were "turnpikes," the term being derived from the large turnstile, made of two timbers, that the toll collector rotated on a post to allow a wagon to pass. The ends of the timbers were usually capped with a metal point and looked something like the pike, a favorite weapon of medieval infantrymen. . . .

Toll roads were indeed profitable investments, and at first private companies built more roads than did local governments. Pennsylvania had the best roads and built the first major gravel road, the Philadelphia-Lancaster turnpike, in 1795. A peddler could get a wagonload of goods to

Lancaster, but he still needed a pack horse to go on to Pittsburgh.

The federal government started a road from Cumberland, Maryland, to Wheeling, West Virginia, to connect the Potomac and Ohio rivers. It was superior to any road built since Roman times. Though it was a winding mountain road, it replaced the trails and footpaths with a sprawling superhighway sixty feet wide. When it opened in 1818, it created a sensation.

With the roads came the taverns and coaching houses, of which the peddler was a frequent visitor, passing along his collection of news, rumors, gossip, and lies as he made his way across the country. The popular image of the colonial and early-American tavern is that of a country inn made of stone, hand-hewn timbers, wide random floorboards, with pretty barmaids and serving wenches, pleasant fires in the nippy weather, tankards of ale, and dinner tables loaded with pheasant and suckling pig. There were, in fact, some splendid taverns, but most were more primitive than charming, and all were overrun with flies, mosquitoes, and vermin. . . .

As the thousands of miles of turnpikes were built, a demand for wagons created a new industry. The peddlers got wagons and loaded them until they creaked. Hugh Auchincloss (a forefather of Hugh D., stepfather of Jacqueline Kennedy Onassis) drove a mule team and wagon loaded with dry goods from New York to Louisville, peddling his way through the War of 1812, ending a "rich man," and becoming another of those "people you never heard of" who rose to wealth and affluence. . . .

As new products appeared, they were added to the tin peddler's wagon until it was a traveling store filled with baskets, books, brooms, brushes, candles, chairs, clocks, cutlery, drugs, hats, jewelry, nursery stock, patent medicines, pins, razors, shoes, silverware, spinning wheels, yarn, and woodenware, to name only part of the list

The South did not participate in the industrial expansion or the road building. God had given them fields instead of factories, and rivers instead of roads, and they were quite content with His choices. The tobacco culture of the South created a small planter class that took a disdainful attitude toward business, and left to the Yankees the crass pursuits of commerce, with the result that until comparatively recent times, the South remained a marketplace for goods manufactured in the Northeast.

Different businesses bred different temperaments, or vice versa, and the resulting personalities were incompatible. The animosity between North and South can be seen in the antagonisms between the Yankee peddler and his southern customers. [According to C. M. Andrews in *Colonial Folkways*] the reputation for hospitality, good breeding, and politeness struck the peddler as a farce acted out by ruthless slaveholders, more accurately noted, it seemed to him, for "their looseness of morals, and their fondness for horse racing, drinking and gambling."

On the other hand, the Southerner felt that the New Englander was full of "pretended holiness and disagreeable self-righteousness . . . [and] criticized his Yankee shrewdness and charged him with business methods that were little short of thievery."

Others disapproved of the peddler, and they weren't all from the South. Dr. Timothy Dwight, president of Yale in 1823, declared that the Yankee peddlers had parted with all modesty and principle. Young men away from home were too free from restraining influences, and their moral decline was certain. It is a measure of his status that the peddler was denounced by so distinguished a critic.

Whether he was hero or villain, the tin peddler was America's leading traveling salesman, and no one saw more of the country than he did, except perhaps the clock peddler.

A legend in his own time, the clock peddler was probably the first traveling salesman who had to justify the need for his product. The tin peddler's wares caught the woman's eye while he was still coming up the road. Tinware was inexpensive and useful, as were the many other things the tin peddler carried. But the clock was an expensive item, somewhat superfluous in homes when the time that mattered most was the time of year. In the selling of clocks, fact and fiction were woven into the legend of Sam Slick, Yankee clock peddler. Sam Slick was the creation of Thomas Haliburton, a Nova Scotian, and was widely enjoyed here and in London as a satire of Yankee gall and cunning. Sam Slick's favorite selling technique was to leave a clock with a family under some pretense, so they might become accustomed to it, and therefore unwilling to give it up. After complimenting the farmer on his land, his crops, his good sense, and flattering the wife with anything that came into his head, he would ask if he might not leave a clock with them for a few weeks while he did some traveling. It was his best clock, he lied, the last of its kind, and it was already sold anyway and he did not want it damaged. As Sam Slick explained, "We trust to soft sawder to get them into the house, and to human natur' that they never come out of it."

Eli Terry did, in fact, sell his clocks with this technique. On one occasion, Terry had in mind a wealthy farmer he knew who might be a likely prospect for a good clock. During a heavy rainstorm Terry rode out to the farmer's house and explained that he had been caught in the rain and feared that his clock would be damaged. He asked if he might not leave it on the farmer's mantel, where it would be safe and dry until he returned from his trip. When Terry returned, the farmer was ready to buy the clock, or more accurately, he was unwilling to part with it. The "free home trial," still popular with merchandisers today, is nothing more than a variation of this clock peddler's trick.

Terry was so successful as a clock peddler that he set up a factory which, he announced, was going to produce one thousand clocks a year. His disbelieving neighbors thought he was mad. How could he make that many clocks? And how on earth could he ever sell them? Within a few years

Terry was producing and selling four thousand clocks a year, and at the time of his death in 1852, Terry left to his sons a factory with an annual production of ten to twelve thousand clocks. . . .

Clock peddlers knocked on a lot of cabin doors and did some fast talking to move that many clocks a year, and altogether they were a pretty wily group. There are many stories of the peddler selling clocks that ran just long enough for him to get his wagon out of sight. Clock-peddler yarns make good reading, but they don't tell the whole story. The descendant of a Bristol clockmaker disputed the traditional view of "these early traveling salesmen." Priscilla Carrington Kline discovered a packet of letters written by clock peddlers to her great grandfather between 1831 and 1842. [In an article in *New England Quarterly*] she particularly took exception to Wright's comment that the peddler was "a commercial bird of passage. He always left his customers convinced and satisfied with their share of the bargain, but he usually managed to clear out after finishing a deal."

Actually, as these letters make clear, the peddler often had to wait a year for his money when the crops were bad, spent idle months without income when shipments were held up, accepted payment in money of doubtless or uncertain value, and had no recourse if the customer refused to make good on his debts, since peddling was often illegal anyway, and where it wasn't, the peddler was at a disadvantage. Justice was not always uniform, being tipped slightly in favor of the resident over the transient. Some of the debts had been standing so long "that one half of the people have smartmouthed, and the balance have forgotten that they ever made such a contract. . .".

As for the money he could collect, the peddler was relieved if he could get it home before its value fluctuated wildly. Wrote one peddler, ". . . we are compelled to take Tenn Alabama and Mississippi paper and a large portion of the latter otherwise we can get nothing at all . . . There is more Shinplaster [unsecured or poorly secured paper money] in circulation in this country than would cover the Kentucky purchase one inch thick."

Sylas Holbrook, who peddled around the country in the 1820s and wrote a book about it [*Sketches by a Traveler*], took an equally dim view of hinterland paper. "I have in my hand a roll that would excite envy, if not suspicion," he wrote, "that would buy little more than a dinner."

The long waits for shipments, the long distance traveled between sales, bad credit, damaged goods, all added to the cost of the products sold by peddlers. As the 1800s neared the halfway mark, the railroads began to ship goods. They were putting some canals out of business almost before the digging had stopped.

While the peddler often used the canalboat as a means of transportation, the development of the canal systems tended to drive peddlers away, deeper into the interior, where goods were scarce.

The canal barge had, only a few years before, replaced the Conestoga wagon as the principal carrier of freight. Now the railroad was taking over. As the railroads extended their tracks, towns and stores grew at every crossing. There were more places to buy things, more things to buy, and at better prices and of more reliable quality than the peddler could supply. Many Yankee peddlers left the road and settled along the way to open a store. Some went back home and began to manufacture the things they had learned by experience that people wanted to buy.

By about 1840, the Yankees were leaving the business in droves. Simultaneously, the immigration of German Jews was increasing rapidly, and they found peddling a way to get their start in the new country. It has been suggested that the Jews, hard-pressed and desperate, had driven the Yankees out of the peddling business. The truth is that the Jews filled the jobs the Yankees were leaving.

The story of the Jewish peddler is a rich history of its own. Many, if not most, of the German Jews who came to the United States around 1840 took up the peddler's pack.

They traveled by foot or by wagon over the back roads of the South and the West, graduating with prosperity from pack peddlers and city hawkers to merchants. A few peddlers like the Lehmans, the Seligmans, Adam Gimbel, and Meyer Guggenheim left legends in their wake.

The Yankee peddler's reputation for sharp dealing was inherited by the Jewish peddlers, and it was not long before the Jews were blamed for every bit of Yankee connivance.

A great deal has been written about the peddler as American history's most unforgettable character, yet he was not just another colorful footnote to America's past. He was the best example of the new man created in the New World. The Puritan and the pioneer have come to symbolize the American experience, but the peddler was closer to possessing all the qualities of the New American than any of the characters of the colonial era. The peddler was resourceful and energetic. He was a "self-starter" who braved all the hardships and terrors that faced the pioneers, and he did it with a pack on his back. When conditions at home did not suit him, the young man who chose the peddler's wandering life displayed the American preference for mobility over quiet resignation at home. Because of . . . willingness to venture out on his own, peddlers were among the first men in the new country to rise from rags to riches, a feat then still new in the world. An ordinary man, with no special endowments, could accumulate wealth, possessing only the desire to do so and the willingness to do the work and run the risks. Skills were not necessary, nor influential friends, or noble birth. The American Dream was born with the peddler.

Businessmen today treat their commercial forefathers as they would a great-grandmother who had been a streetwalker. They might consider, however, that the colonization of the United States was a commercial venture underwritten by stock companies for a profit, and that commerce turned more wheels than did the quest for religious freedom or the flight from tyranny. We were the children of international trade and we grew up, as a country, buying and selling, although we don't like to think of ourselves in quite this way.

From the time of the Pilgrims, selling was an art that began to acquire distinctly American characteristics. Assuming the overtones of a religion and a science, it was infused into the American man in the colonial crucible in which he was formed. He was born with the soul of a salesman—and a traveling salesman, at that.

"The American tradition," wrote Max Lerner, "has grown by movement, not by sitting." It grew from a restless people, possessed by their energy, pursuing their dreams with quickening hope. It was not natural to our tradition to sit and wait when every impulse said go and get. The peddler was in step with the mood of the times, and the territory he chose was as magnetic to him as the frontier. In fact, in most cases, it *was* the frontier.

TRAVELING PLAYERS[7]

"There is much discourse now of beginning stage plays in New England," Increase Mather [Congregational clergyman, president of Harvard] wrote in 1686, at a time when the Puritan power seemed supreme. The restless interest in the theater worked slowly, with long gaps between its triumphs, but it was unremitting. By 1750 Bostonians were so eager to see a play at a coffee-house that a serious riot took place at its doors. Soon after the Revolution an exquisite theater was built in Boston, designed by [Charles] Bulfinch [American architect] and containing a chastely ornamented dancing-room, card rooms, and tea rooms. In eastern cities of the coast from New York to Charleston, playhouses were established; and as the migration from New England moved westward into upper New York, into western Pennsylvania

[7] From *American Humor* by Constance Rourke, biographer and historian. Harcourt. '31. p 106–15. Copyright, 1931 by Harcourt Brace Jovanovich, Inc; copyright, 1959, by Alice D. Fore. Reprinted by permission of the publishers.

and . . . [Ohio], theatricals seemed to spring up in their wake. By 1815 small companies had reached Kentucky, and improvised theaters soon dotted the West. In the little town of Columbus in Georgia, timber that waved in the breeze on Monday was transformed into a theater the following Thursday. In Natchez a theater was built in an old graveyard, with dressing-rooms beneath the stage like catacombs, and bones in view. Ballrooms of plantation mansions were fitted up for performances, and plays were performed in taverns.

In the West at least, on the frontier, where the mixed elements of the American character were taking a pronounced shape, the results were hardly considerable as drama. The best acting—and many gifted players traveled over the country—could offer little more than sheer theatricals. With transient audiences and scratch companies and the hardships of travel there was small chance for intensification and depth; even the elder Booth concentrated only on single scenes. The pioneer theater was coarsened and haphazard. No drama came out of this broad movement: nothing can be clearer than the fact that drama as a powerful native form did not appear in America at this time or even throughout the entire nineteenth century. But the theatrical seemed a native mode. The Yankee first fully emerged in the theater; each of the trio of native characters was seen there. The theater took a place which in a civilization of slower and quieter growth might have been occupied almost altogether by casual song and story; even the comic tale was theatrically contrived, with the teller always the actor, and the effect dependent upon manner and gesture and the stress of speech.

Now the theatrical, as opposed to the dramatic, is full of experiment, finding its way to audiences by their quick responses and rejections. On the stage the shimmer and glow, the minor appurtenances, the jokes and dances and songs, the stretching and changes of plots, are arranged and altered almost literally by the audience or in their close company; its measure is human, not literary. The American theater then, particularly in the West, was a composite of native feeling. It had significance, not because it might at some later time evolve into great national art, but because it was closely interwoven with the American character and the American experience. It marched with the forces of dispersal, essaying a hundred things by way of entertainment and revealing a growing temper.

Like gypsy crews, strolling actors moved over the country following the trail of the pioneers, often abreast of them. At Olean one company bought a broadhorn [a large flatboat] and floated down the Alleghany, playing airs from *The Beggar's Opera* at solitary cabins, finding music in abundance wherever a few settlers were gathered. A troupe stopped at a double log cabin and discovered that a tiny theater had been contrived in a loft, with curtains and three large benches for boxes and pit. There with a few crude properties they offered the semblance of romance: but the world which they created for a few hours was no more fanciful than that which existed in the minds of their small audience. All around them lay shadowy sites of public buildings and wide ephemeral avenues and streets. . . .

Many companies went into the West by way of the Alleghany, leaving behind them white flags flying on the banks of the river at places where those who followed might find a friendly reception. Pittsburgh, "sunk in sin and sea-coal," where pioneers had often been stranded for lack of money or had suffered strange adventures, was a difficult crossroads for actors. Not many of them could match the inhabitants in conviviality. One complained, "To see a Pittsburgh *bon vivant* under the table is a task few attempt who know them, and fewer succeed in accomplishing." And when debt was involved, difficulties in Pittsburgh were doubled. "The constables of Pittsburgh never forget an old friend," mourned the people of the theater. "What actor who has visited this

city will ever forget it?" they cried satirically. As one actor
was playing the gravedigger in *Hamlet,* he saw the bailiffs
in the wings and popped into the grave, and was never
heard of again. A whole troupe was caught on the wing for
debt as they tried to leave town, and were obliged to hire
themselves out as waxworks at a museum to raise the necessary money. A celebrated few succeeded in slipping away in
skiffs down the Ohio at night.

In rafts, in broadhorns, companies traveled down the
Ohio and the Mississippi, stopping at the larger cities, often
playing in small villages. Some went on by wagon into the
hills of Kentucky, where the roads were so steep that they
were obliged to unload their properties and carry them, and
where they often left their watches and chains behind as
toll. A few passed through the Cumberland Gap and thus
to Richmond, then coastwise to Savannah and farther south.
One troupe ventured into Florida during the Seminole War,
playing at forts and garrisons on the way, threatened by
the Indians but continuing their journey until they were
finally set upon, some of their number killed, and their
wardrobe seized. Thereafter for a time the Seminoles gal-
loped through the sandy lowlands garbed as Romans, High-
landers, and Shakespearean heroes.

Some companies deployed through Kentucky and Tennessee to the Gulf States, traveling down crooked little
rivers in overladen steamers that took on cotton at every
wharf, with Negroes pushing huge bales of cotton over the
bluffs at night by the light of great fires and with a pit of
fire roaring in the steamer below. Everywhere they found
theaters, or theaters were improvised for them; everyone
came, black and white, children and their elders. Backwoodsmen rode up in their fringes and green blankets and
fur. Flatboatmen could be distinguished by their rolling
stride and implacable manner. Planters appeared in white
Spanish hats of beaver on fine horses with bright saddle-
cloths, and farmers with their wives on pillions [a cushion

attached behind a saddle for an extra rider], and a host of Negroes.

Off stage the actors maintained an air of urban elegance, highly keyed, with coats of a lighter blue, green, or brown than was usually worn, and hats a little larger or smaller than was the custom. For the stage they brought baskets of faded velvet and silken finery; often their adornments were scant or contrived. One manager never permitted his actors the luxury of fleshings [flesh-colored tights], but painted their legs and his own buff, red, or white for tragedy, with stripes and spots for comedy. Many an actor had for his theatrical wardrobe only a flaxen wig and a pair of comic stockings. The companies were small. Everybody doubled. Everyone had precarious adventures.

In a theater at Mobile a slight noise was heard in one of the upper boxes, a rush, a bit of scuffle; the ladies in the box did not move; in the crowded pit there was almost no sensation, though it was soon clear that a man had been knifed. The performance and the applause proceeded without a break. Ambuscades were sometimes set on the roads for the actors; they were always dodging epidemics of cholera or escaping from fires. Yet they continued to join in that perpetual travel which often seemed the single enduring feature of the country. As processions of families and slaves moved from the Carolinas and Georgia to some new tract of forest or canebrake, the actors were close at their heels. . . . [With the invention of the showboat, actors] went up the Arkansas River to wild country, encountering ruffians, sometimes besieged, dealing out grape and canister in return, but inured to the life and continuing to ply the rivers for years.

By their own wish and in the fancy of their audiences these people of the theater remained a caste apart. The theater still savored of the black arts even though the ban upon it was broken. Changes of character on the stage seemed not altogether different from those which the devil was supposed to assume, changes of scene not far from black magic. These actors could change you "a forest into a front parlor, a desert into a dining-room, a stormy ocean into a flower garden, a palace into a den of thieves, all on the sound of a boatswain's whistle." Yet intangibly they joined with the people and the region, their bold accents of dress and posture heightening the native drift in that direction, their romantic language mingling with the stressed speech of the backwoods.

In an imaginative sense the audiences of the backwoods joined deeply with the players. Theirs was that intimate participation which means that acting has become reality. Out of the forest, groups would come riding at night who would talk with the actors as the play proceeded, or with each other about the characters. On a small stage in a Kentucky village a gambler's family was pictured as starving, and a countryman rose from one of the boxes. "I propose we make up something for this woman," he said. Someone whispered that it was all a sham, but he delivered a brief discourse on the worthlessness of the gambler, flung a bill on the stage with his pocketbook, advised the woman not to let her husband know about it or he would spend it all on faro, and then with a divided mind sat down, saying, "Now go on with the play."

Such participation often meant deep and direct drafts upon the emotions, and the black romantical plays like *Pizarro, The Iron Chest,* and *Venice Preserved,* popular at this time, with their themes of envy, hatred, remorse, terror, revenge, could evoke an emotional response with force and abundance. The bolder tragedies of Shakespeare—never his comedies in that early day—were staple pieces, with plays of the supernatural. *Hamlet* was frequently played for the ghost, the murder, the burial, and *Macbeth* for the witches, the sleep-walking scene, and the knocking at the gate, so strongly did the pioneer taste lean in this direction. Since lights were scarce the effects were eerie. One company acted a tragedy wholly in the dark before a Kentucky mountain audience. *The Spectre Bridegroom* was played by moonlight in a low-roofed opening like a hallway between two cabins, and the ballet of *The Wizard Skiff* was danced before guttering candles. Hushed and startled, these audiences would watch and listen; then again the low murmuring talk would begin among themselves or with the actors.

Here in disguised and transmuted forms emotions which had been dominant in the early day of the pioneer lived again—emotions stirred by a sense of the supernatural, and those grosser feelings begotten of a primitive conflict between man and man, or of man and a rude destiny. With these came the wraith of the Indian.

As the Indian perished or was driven farther and farther from those fertile lands which the white invader wished to occupy, a noble and mournful fantasy was created in his place. After the Revolution, Indian plays and operas abounded. From the 1820s onward [James Fenimore] Cooper followed with a spate of Indian novels. In the 1830s, when the trio of popular American figures appeared at full length, the Indian assumed a still loftier stature and a more tragic mien. These were the first palmy years of [Edwin] Forrest's appearance in *Metamora, the Last of the Wampanoags,* a play whose vogue seemed unremitting, and which was copied in dozens of less conspicuous successes. Cooper's *Wept of the Wish Ton Wish* was dramatized and even became a ballet. The stage soon overflowed with Indian figures. Painted and decked, the dusky hero went his tragic way, fighting to be sure, full of "carnivorous rages" when Forrest played the parts, but most often declaiming. The Indian's pride, his grief, his lost inheritance, his kinship with the boundless wilderness, were made enduring themes. Talk flowed again in Indian monologues, in oratorical outbursts, in rhapsodies.

This fantastic Indian was subjective, white beneath the war-paint, springing into full stature when pioneer life was receding. About his figure the American seemed to wrap a desire to return to the primitive life of the wilderness. It

was not for nothing that he had appropriated Indian methods of warfare, Indian costumes, Indian legends: this borrowing had left a wide imprint. In the Indian plays he could
drench himself in melancholy remembrance of the time
when the whole continent was untouched. These plays were
mournful elegies, and it would be easy to call them proof
of national hypocrisy. But a whole people will hardly pore
over books and drive themselves to the theater for more
than thirty years in order to build up an effective attitude
which no one is at hand to see but themselves; nor will
they do so to smother a collective conscience. Like the
novels of Cooper, the plays were immensely popular; and
their elegiac sentiment surged up in a region where a more
realistic view might have been expected to prevail, in the
West. It was there that the legendary Indian strutted and
declaimed and mourned with the greatest vigor, on small
rude stages, before audiences of small farmers and backwoodsmen. He seemed an improbable and ghostly ancestor.

LIFE ON AN IOWA FARM [8]

The early seventies were years of swift change on the
Middle Border. Day by day the settlement thickened. Section by section the prairie was blackened by the plow.
Month by month the sweet wild meadows were fenced and
pastured and so at last the colts and cows all came into
captivity, and our horseback riding ceased, cut short as if
by some imperial decree. Lanes of barbed wire replaced the
winding wagon trails, our saddles gathered dust in the
grain-sheds, and groves of Lombardy poplar and European
larch replaced the tow-heads of aspen and hazel through
which we had pursued the wolf and fox.

I will not say that this produced in me any keen sense

[8] From *A Son of the Middle Border*, by Hamlin Garland (1860–1940), American novelist and man of letters. Text from Macmillan edition. 10th ptg 1961.
p 144, 147–51, 152–3, 155–8. Copyright 1917 by Hamlin Garland, renewed 1945
by Mary I. Lord and Constance G. Williams. Reprinted with permission of Macmillan Publishing Co., Inc.

of sorrow at the time, for though I missed our horse-herds and the charm of the open spaces, I turned to tamer sports with the resilient adaptability of youth. If I could not ride I could at least play baseball, and the swimming hole in the Little Cedar remained untouched. The coming in of numerous Eastern settlers brought added charm to neighborhood life. Picnics, conventions, Fourth of July celebrations —all intensified our interest, and in their increasing drama we were compensated, in some degree at least, for the delights which were passing with the prairie. . . .

As I look back over my life on that Iowa farm the song of the reaper fills large place in my mind. We were all worshipers of wheat in those days. The men thought and talked of little else between seeding and harvest, and you will not wonder at this if you have known and bowed before such abundance as we then enjoyed.

Deep as the breast of a man, wide as the sea, heavy-headed, supple-stocked, many-voiced, full of multitudinous, secret, whispered colloquies—a meeting place of winds and of sunlight—our fields ran to the world's end.

We trembled when the storm lay hard upon the wheat, we exulted as the lilac shadows of noonday drifted over it! We went out into it at noon when all was still—so still we could hear the pulse of the transforming sap as it crept from cool root to swaying plume. We stood before it at evening when the setting sun flooded it with crimson, the bearded heads lazily swirling under the wings of the wind, the mousing hawk dipping into its green deeps like the eagle into the sea, and our hearts expanded with the beauty and the mystery of it—and back of all this was the knowledge that its abundance meant a new carriage, an addition to the house, or a new suit of clothes.

Haying was over, and day by day we boys watched with deepening interest while the hot sun transformed the juices of the soil into those stately stalks. I loved to go out into the fairy forest of it, and lying there, silent in its swaying deeps, hear the wild chickens peep and the wind sing its subtle song over our heads. Day by day I studied the barley as it turned yellow, first at the root and then at the neck (while the middle joints, rank and sappy, retained their blue-green sheen), until at last the lower leaves began to wither and the stems to stiffen in order to uphold the daily increasing weight of the milky berries, and then almost in an hour—lo! the edge of the field became a banded ribbon of green and yellow, languidly waving in and out with every rush of the breeze.

Now we got out the reaper, put the sickles in order, and Father laid in a store of provisions. Extra hands were hired, and at last, early on a hot July morning, the boss mounted to his seat on the self-rake McCormick and drove into the field. Frank rode the lead horse, four stalwart hands and myself took stations behind the reaper, and the battle was on!

Reaping generally came about the 20th of July, the hottest and dryest part of the summer, and was the most pressing work of the year. It demanded early rising for the men, and it meant an all-day broiling over the kitchen stove for the women. Stern, incessant toil went on inside and out from dawn till sunset, no matter how the thermometer sizzled. On many days the mercury mounted to ninety-five in the shade, but with wide fields all yellowing at the same moment, no one thought of laying off. A storm might sweep it flat, or if neglected too long it might crinkle.

Our reaper in 1874 was a new model of the McCormick self-rake—the Marsh harvester was not yet in general use. The Woods dropper, the Seymour and Morgan hand-rake contraptions, seemed a long way in the past. True, the McCormick required four horses to drag it, but it was effective. It was hard to believe that anything more cunning would ever come to claim the farmer's money. Weird tales of a machine on which two men rode and bound twelve acres of wheat in ten hours came to us, but we did not potently believe these reports—on the contrary we accepted the self-rake as quite the final word in harvesting machinery and cheerily bent to the binding of sheaves with their own straw in the good old time-honored way.

No task save that of cradling surpassed in severity binding on a station. It was a full-grown man's job, but every boy was ambitious to try his hand, and when at fourteen years of age I was promoted from bundle boy to be one of the five hands to bind after the reaper, I went to my corner with joy and confidence. For two years I had been serving as binder on the corners (to keep the grain out of the way of the horses), and I knew my job.

I was short and broad-shouldered, with large, strong hands admirably adapted for this work, and for the first two hours easily held my own with the rest of the crew; but as the morning wore on and the sun grew hotter my enthusiasm waned. A painful void developed in my chest. My breakfast had been ample, but no mere stomachful of food could carry a growing boy through five hours of desperate toil. Along about a quarter to ten I began to scan the field with anxious eye, longing to see Harriet and the promised luncheon basket.

Just when it seemed that I could endure the strain no longer she came bearing a jug of cool milk, some cheese, and some deliciously fresh friedcakes. With keen joy I set a couple of tall sheaves together like a tent and flung myself down flat on my back in their shadow to devour my lunch.

Tired as I was, my dim eyes apprehended something of the splendor of the shining clouds which rolled like storms of snow through the deep blue spaces of sky, and so, resting silently as a clod, I could hear the chirp of the crickets, the buzzing wings of flies, and the faint, fairylike tread of smaller unseen insects hurrying their way just beneath my ear in the stubble. Strange green worms, grasshoppers, and shining beetles crept over me as I dozed.

This delicious, dreamful respite was broken by the far-off approaching purr of the sickle, flicked by the faint snap of the driver's whip, and out of the low rustle of the ever-stirring Lilliputian forest came the wailing cry of a baby wild chicken lost from its mother—a falling, thrilling, piteous little pipe.

Such momentary communion with nature seemed all the sweeter for the work which had preceded it as well as that which was to follow it. It took resolution to rise and go back to my work, but I did it, sustained by a kind of soldierly pride.

At noon we hurried to the house, surrounded the kitchen table, and fell upon our boiled beef and potatoes with such ferocity that in fifteen minutes our meal was over. There was no ceremony and very little talking till the hid wolf was appeased. Then came a heavenly half hour of rest on the cool grass in the shade of the trees, a siesta as luxurious as that of a Spanish monarch—but alas!—this "nooning," as we called it, was always cut short by Father's words of sharp command: "Roll out, boys!" and again the big white jugs were filled at the well, the horses, lazy with food, led the way back to the field, and the stern contest began again.

All nature at this hour seemed to invite to repose rather than to labor, and as the heat increased I longed with word-less fervor for the green woods of the Cedar River. At times the gentle wind hardly moved the bended heads of the barley, and the hawks hung in the air like trout sleeping in deep pools. The sunlight was a golden, silent, scorching cataract—yet each of us must strain his tired muscles and bend his aching back to the harvest.

Supper came at five, another delicious interval—and then at six we all went out again for another hour or two in the cool of the sunset. However, the pace was more leisurely now, for the end of the day was near. I always enjoyed this period, for the shadows lengthening across the stubble and the fiery sun veiled by the gray clouds of the west had won-drous charm. The air began to moisten and grow cool. The voices of the men pulsed powerfully and cheerfully across the narrowing field of unreaped grain, the prairie hens led forth their broods to feed, and at last, Father's long-drawn and musical cry: "Turn out! All hands TURN OUT!" rang with restful significance through the dusk. Then, slowly, with low-hung heads the freed horses moved toward the barn, walking with lagging steps like weary warriors going into camp. . . .

The reaping on our farm that year lasted about four weeks. Barley came first, wheat followed, the oats came last of all. No sooner was the final swath cut than the barley was ready to be put under cover, and stacking, a new and less exacting phase of the harvest, began.

This job required less men than reaping; hence a part of our hands were paid off; only the more responsible ones were retained. The rush, the strain, of the reaping gave place to a leisurely, steady, day-by-day garnering of the thoroughly seasoned shocks into great conical piles, four in a place in the midst of the stubble, which was already growing green with swiftly springing weeds.

A full crew consisted of a stacker, a boy to pass bundles, two drivers for the heavy wagon racks, and a pitcher in the field who lifted the sheaves from the shock with a three-tined fork and threw them to the man on the load.

At the age of ten I had been taught to handle bundles on the stack, but now at fourteen I took my father's place as stacker, whilst he passed the sheaves and told me how to lay them. This exalted me at the same time that it increased my responsibility. It made a man of me—not only in my own estimation, but in the eyes of my boy companions, to whom I discoursed loftily on the value of "bulges" and the advantages of the stack over the rick.

No sooner was the stacking ended than the dreaded task of plowing began for Burton and John and me. Every morning while our fathers and the hired men shouldered their forks and went away to help some neighbor thrash ("changing works"), we drove our teams into the field, there to plod round and round in solitary course. . . .

Franklin's job was almost as lonely. He was set to herd the cattle on the harvested stubble and keep them out of the corn field. A little later, in October, when I was called to take my place as corn husker, he was promoted to the plow. Our only respite during the months of October and November was the occasional cold rain which permitted us to read or play cards in the kitchen. . . .

The crops on our farms in those first years were enormous, and prices were good; and yet the homes of the neighborhood were slow in taking on grace or comfort. I don't know why this was so, unless it was that the men were continually buying more land and more machinery. Our own stables were still straw-roofed sheds, but the trees which we had planted had grown swiftly into a grove, and a garden, tended at odd moments by all hands, brought small fruits and vegetables in season. Although a constantly improving collection of farm machinery lightened the burdens of the husbandman, the drudgery of the housewife's dishwashing and cooking did not correspondingly lessen. I fear it increased, for with the widening of the fields came the doubling of the harvest hands, and my mother continued to do most of the housework herself—cooking, sewing, washing, churning, and nursing the sick from time to time. No one in trouble ever sent for Isabelle Garland in vain, and I have many recollections of neighbors riding up in the night and calling for her with agitated voices.

Of course I did not realize, and I am sure my father did not realize, the heavy burden, the endless grind, of her toil. Harriet helped, of course, and Frank and I churned and carried wood and brought water; but even with such aid, the round of Mother's duties must have been as relentless as a treadmill. Even on Sunday, when we were free for a part of the day, she was required to furnish forth three meals and to help Frank and Jessie dress for church. She sang less and less, and the songs we loved were seldom referred to. If I could only go back for one little hour and take her in my arms and tell her how much I owe her for those grinding days! . . .

Threshing time, which was becoming each year less of a bee and more of a job (many of the men were mere hired hands), was made distinctive by David, who came over from Orchard with his machine—the last time as it turned out—and stayed to the end. As I cut bands beside him in the dust and thunder of the cylinder I regained something of my boyish worship of his strength and skill. The tireless easy swing of his great frame was wonderful to me, and when, in my weariness, I failed to slash a band he smiled and tore the sheaf apart—thus deepening my love for him. I looked up at him at such times as a sailor regards his captain on the bridge. His handsome immobile bearded face, his air of command, his large gestures as he rolled the broad sheaves into the howling maw of the machine, made of him a chieftain.—The touch of melancholy which even then had begun to develop added to his manly charm.

One day in late September as I was plowing in the field at the back of the farm I encountered a particularly troublesome thicket of weeds and vines in the stubble and decided to burn the way before the colter. We had been doing this ever since the frost had killed the vegetation but always on lands after they had been safeguarded by strips of plowing. On this particular land no fire had been set for the reason that four large stacks of wheat still stood waiting the thresher. In my irritation and self-confidence I decided to clear away the matted stubble on the same strip, though at some distance from the stacks. This seemed safe enough at the time, for the wind was blowing gently from the opposite direction.

It was a lovely golden day, and as I stood watching the friendly flame clearing the ground for me, I was filled with satisfaction. Suddenly I observed that the line of red was moving steadily against the wind and *toward* the stacks. My satisfaction changed to alarm. The matted weeds furnished a thick bed of fuel, and against the progress of the flame I had nothing to offer. I could only hope that the thinning stubble would permit me to trample it out. I tore at the ground in desperation, hoping to make a bare spot which the flame could not leap. I trampled the fire with my bare

feet. I beat at it with my hat. I screamed for help. Too late
I thought of my team and the plow with which I might have
drawn a furrow around the stacks. The flame touched the
high-piled sheaves. It ran lightly, beautifully up the sides—
and as I stood watching it, I thought: "It is all a dream. It
can't be true."

But it was. In less than twenty minutes the towering
piles had melted into four glowing heaps of ashes. Four
hundred dollars had gone up in that blaze.

Slowly, painfully I hobbled to the plow and drove my
team to the house. Although badly burned, my mental suffering was so much greater that I felt only part of it. Leaving
the horses at the well, I hobbled into the house to my
mother. She, I knew, would sympathize with me and shield
me from the just wrath of my father, who was away but was
due to return in an hour or two.

Mother received me in silence, bandaged my feet, and
put me to bed, where I lay in shame and terror.

At last I heard father come in. He questioned; Mother's
voice replied. He remained ominously silent. She went on
quietly but with an eloquence unusual in her. What she said
to him I never knew, but when he came up the stairs and
stood looking down at me his anger had cooled. He merely
asked me how I felt, uncovered my burned feet, examined
them, put the sheet back, and went away, without a word
either of reproof or consolation.

OPENING UP OKLAHOMA [9]

ARKANSAS CITY, Kan., April 22, 1889.—Few of the
thousands of seekers of something for nothing, who have
used this city as their last halting place prior to making the
rush into Oklahoma, went to bed last night. They spent the
night on the streets, at the depot, and in and out of hotel
lobbies. Yesterday's influx of visitors was enormous. The

[9] Article entitled "Settling Oklahoma" in the St. Louis *Globe Democrat*, April
23, 1889.

regular trains have had to run in sections. And this extra accommodation has not sufficed. The aisles have been crowded to excess, and the suffering of the cooped-up specu-lators and boomers must have been great. Fortunately there were very few women in the crowds.

The depot was crowded all night, and the sale of tickets kept steadily on, nine tenths of those issued being to Guth-rie and most of the balance to Arthur. This latter is just five miles over the line, and as all trains will stop before leaving the Cherokee strip, the holders of tickets to Arthur propose to jump off at the line. Every one seemed to be talk-ing, and there was a perfect babel, but the grand rush com-menced about six, when the people who had slept uptown joined their less fortunate brethren. Some carried absolutely nothing in their hands, evidently thinking they could do the rushing better for not being handicapped. But a marked characteristic of the crowd was the great number of spades and axes carried. The [railroad] company's arrangements to prevent a general rush to one train was to so arrange matters that no one could know which train could pass first, and the secret has been admirably kept.

The trip south commenced amid shouting and cheering. There could not have been less than five thousand men who failed to secure seats, although a score of flatcars had been fitted up with plank seats, which were crowded with eager boomers.

Two men got on the cowcatcher of a locomotive but had to be removed. On a later train, however, a man rode the whole journey of eighty-nine miles on the cowcatcher. There were only two ladies on the train. Each had a light boomer's outfit and expressed confidence in the gallantry of the men to enable them to locate claims. The conductor collected ten hundred and twenty-four tickets on this train.

At twelve-fifteen precisely there was a loud whistle from the engine, answered by a shout from the train, and we were in Oklahoma at last. Before the train had crossed the line fifty yards a man sprang off, regardless of the danger. He fell pretty heavily but was on his feet in a few seconds, collected his baggage, which he had thrown out ahead, and was turning sods before the train was out of sight. A little farther south a man had evidently just alighted from the mule which was standing by him and whose pack he was unloading. So far it was just possible that every boomer seen had waited till twelve o'clock before he crossed the line, but squatters pure and simple now came in view. They sprang out of the woods on every side, and it was evident from the appearance of some of them that they had been in hiding for weeks. . . .

When the word was given to advance at the north line, the boomers started forward at various rates of speed. All who desired to locate anywhere near the track in the north end of the Territory found themselves forestalled. Some turned back in disgust, and others pushed farther on into the interior. But for absolute contempt of the President's reminder of the dangers of premature occupation, Guthrie takes the lead. It could not legally be reached by road in advance of the train; yet when the town site came in view, it was literally covered with lot claimants. The location is well suited for a town. The railroad runs along a valley on the west of which is a creek which forms a picturesque background to the depot. The town, or town site, is on the other side of the track; and the ground slopes gradually up to the summit of a little ridge. At the summit is the land office.

What happened when the train began to slacken beggars all description. Boys, middle-aged men, and old fellows threw themselves off the platform and commenced a wild rush. They fell upon each other, scrambled to their feet, and made off, some carrying their grips and others dropping everything in the eagerness of the chase. As the train went on toward the depot the passengers kept jumping off. The town-lot craze seemed to lend speed even to cripples. A man with a wooden leg was among the first to make the dangerous jump, and he held his own in the race. Not a passenger by this first train went past Guthrie, so that the population of the new city was increased by this rush to the extent of nearly a thousand. All roads seemed to lead to the land office at which a line over one hundred yards long was already formed. For a second the runners paused.

Then they commenced a wild tear out east, and each man, as he found an unclaimed lot, proceeded to stake it out and hold it down. The process of securing the lots, as in general adoption, is simple in the extreme. First of all a stake is driven in the ground, with or without a placer attached, setting forth the name of the claimant. Then the new owner paces off the ground he proposes to occupy for a residence or business house. There is at least a charm of variety about the laying out of Guthrie. Some people contented themselves with twenty-five feet frontage, others took forty feet, and others fifty; but most of the claimants had a fair idea of where the streets ought to be and left the necessary space for them. By the time the men on Train No. 1 had each selected his lot the town site had extended away beyond the half section reserved, and long before the majority had quit running, Train No. 2 pulled in, quite as heavily loaded as its predecessor. The same process was carried out to the letter.

Among those hurrying up the hill were two ladies who succeeded in securing a claim each and will hold it. These ladies are from California. They are going into business at once.

There was a considerable interval before another train arrived, but the third and fourth came in close together, each discharging its cargo of passengers to add to the astounding crush. The limits of the city kept on increasing, and by the time the fifth and sixth trains had unloaded, the city extended far away to the distance. Altogether ten trains got in before three o'clock, and making allowance for those who went on to Oklahoma City, there must have been at least six thousand people in Guthrie three hours after the Territory was legally opened for settlement. It was wonderful, the manner in which disputes among the newcomers were settled in this early part of the proceedings. Sometimes half a dozen men would pounce on a lot simultaneously or nearly so. Each would commence to stake out, but after a little while a general agreement would be come to, and every applicant but one would rush off and secure an undisputed lot. There has been so far no unpleasantness of any kind.

Speculation in town lots commenced at once. Hacks met the trains and drivers shouted, "This way for lots at a dollar apiece!"

For a dollar lot hunters were driven to vacant lots and left to get their dollar's worth themselves.

II. THE TWENTIETH CENTURY PICTURE

EDITORS' INTRODUCTION

Today, at a little past the three-quarter mark of the twentieth century, perhaps it is possible to draw some comparisons between this and the nineteenth century. By now, the split between modern industrialized, technological, urbanized American life and the earlier American ideal of independence and self-sufficiency, relying primarily on the soil and hard work, has become a gulf. However, some trends are developing and will continue to develop in the last quarter of this century that combine the advantages of living nearer the earth with some of the technological advances of recent decades.

All of the extracts in this section were written between 1934 and 1975. The first three present contrasting pictures. In *Backwoods America,* Charles M. Wilson, a native of the Ozarks, describes various aspects of life in that area in the 1930s, concentrating on the human advantages of the simple life, much the way Thoreau did a hundred years earlier. The hard side of rural life is shown by Frederick Lewis Allen, writing in 1939. He recounts the miseries resulting from drought and flood.

The next articles are from the 1950s. Two selections from Max Lerner's *America as a Civilization* examine farm and small-town life from a sociological point of view. Then, D. W. Brogan, the British historian and political scientist who wrote widely on American life, discusses the disproportionate political power of American agricultural interests in the national legislative bodies. Both writers deal with the paradox of the independent farmer who prizes his "masterless state" but is the beneficiary of large-scale economic support from the federal government.

The concluding articles are from the seventies. The first

by Roe C. Black, executive editor of *Farm Journal,* explains how ethnic characteristics from the Old World cross-pollinated in America's rich land to make an agriculture of unprecedented productivity. The second, by John Walsh of *Science,* deals with the development of agribusiness and the evolving relationship of grain and processing corporations to individual farmers.

AMERICAN PEASANTS [1]

I know a land of Elizabethan ways, an America of cavaliers and curtsies, a land of mystic allegiances and enduring frontiers, where moods of yesterday touch hands with probable ways of tomorrow. Smooth, timbered hills painted green-golden by the magic of sunlight. Hillsides and green valleys, lost ravines and forest lands. Clear rivers, fast running and gay. Farm roads that smile in good fellowship. Fence-rows, open fields, and a comforting, life-giving earth.

As my neighbor Bill Coldiron puts it, "Life is good hereabouts, because a man don't keep eternally in a sweat about things."

I am speaking of my homeland, the backhill Ozarks of Arkansas and Missouri. This particular haven of peasantry happens to be my America. It is a centrally placed stronghold for proprietary farms and homestead living. During my pleasurable years of association with this and other rural Americas, I have become thoroughly convinced that Ozarkadia provides a splendid laboratory from which to study the true living ways and resources of the nation's peasant domain. If I am certain of anything at all, I am certain that good yeomen the country over, for that matter the world over, hold a vast deal in common. So I ponder upon this peasantry, confident that I am close to the true heart of

[1] From *Backwoods America,* by Charles Morrow Wilson, journalist and specialist on rural America. University of North Carolina Press. '34. Excerpts from p 1–11, 119–24. Reprinted by permission of the author.

agrarian America; for mine is a world that is today and yesterday and very probably tomorrow, all in one.

Hereabouts, farm people are long-settled descendants of first immigrants from Elizabethan England, a nation of life coming into full prime. Husbandmen and plowmen of Shakespeare's England could very probably rub shoulders and swap yarns with them, and suffer few misunderstandings, lingual or otherwise.

"All the corn we make our bread of, groweth on our own demesne ground. The flesh we eat is all (or the most part) of our own breeding. Our garments, also, or much thereof, made within our house. Our own malt and water maketh our drink."

Thus went an English country gentleman's boast of self-sufficiency over three and a half centuries ago. Hereabouts, it is much the same. The landholder gambles squarely upon the benevolence of soil, growth, and weather. He plants, hunts, and harvests with the basic idea of self-sufficiency. His wife cooks, churns, makes the clothes, and keeps the home. . . .

In Ozarkadia, as in various other peasant realms, October brings the corn harvest and the end of the tenant's year. But tilling is usually finished by early August and so corn huskings, county fairs, and circuses provide the uplander autumnal daytime diversion. Then comes the regular run of the season's merry-making—play-parties, dances, quiltings, housewarmings, candy pulling, 'possum hunts.

The life is essentially a matter of sunshine and storm, growth and rest, the progress of seasons, the changing of skies, transactions of the long-established firm of Sun, Rain, and Earth. The basic hypotheses are bounded by apples and firewood, a smoke-house full of pork joints, a crib of corn, and a treasury of chewing tobacco for the winter.

Oldish ways linger. Surface soil is washed away by riotous spring floods. Bridle paths are washed into gulleys. Old roads pass into grass-grown oblivion. There are abandoned villages, and villages lost, gray citadels of hay carts and strolling pigs. In a way it is an old man's country, a civilization begun by hands long in the grave.

Yet it is also a frontier, enduring and invincible, a country of landowning, small-acreage farmers who treat life well and who are treated well by life. Its people continue to make livings from the soil, just as they have been doing since the first coming of white pioneers, and just as they likely will be doing when our grandchildren are tottering old men. . . .

Old ways live on in the farther back spaces. Oldtimers live out enjoyable years without getting many miles from their birthplaces. Bill Coldiron, who lives just up the lane from me, has done considerable thinking about distances and places. Bill allows that when he dies he would naturally like to go to heaven. But in course of ethereal transit, he would relish a brief detour to either Little Rock or St. Louis, which would give a chance for looking over a city.

There is still a scattering of good Americans who never used a telephone. Uncle Homer Mullinix from down on Hazel Creek never had. One day he tramped into Fayetteville to make his will, and the old lawyer let him have a try at the phone. Uncle Homer proceeded to call over the cow-pasture line to the Brentwood store, where his wife had gone for a turn of groceries. Just as he took down the receiver, lightning struck the wire.

"Yass, it's her all right!" . . .

True, it is a frontier that holds such modern realities as numbered highways, ventilated schoolhouses, automobiles, wayside markets and lighted streets. The towns have colleges, arcades, and depots. But the towns are almost entirely dependent upon farming realms and backhills, not only for their commercial life, but for the lion's share of their human interest. Earth and men build the dominating interest.

The country is not new to settlement. Its farm lands have given nurture and fair lives to five or six generations of land tillers. But it has kept its frontier temperament. In saying this, I repeat that to me "frontier" involves a double assumption: first, plentiful and readily available farm land; secondly, a widespread craving to occupy such land, plus a willingness to till and cherish the land when it is taken.

In this backwoods America, which is surprisingly large and far-spread, you may be wandering along a farm road which shows no intentions of going anywhere in particular, when all at once the road widens and there you are in Red Star, or Nellie's Apron, or Eagle Rock, or some other unmapped hamlet. You usually know the town by its store, since the store is very likely the town as well.

Bill Burg has kept a crossroads store at Compton, Arkansas, for forty-nine years. The chances are that you have never been to Compton, Arkansas. Further, that you couldn't find it on a map, unless the map were a very big and complete one. But Compton is nevertheless a reality. Bill Burg started the village when he started his store. Now it has two other stores and a schoolhouse.

We seated ourselves on a counter beneath an overhanging stock of assorted lamp chimneys, baking soda, and axe handles. A hound dog waited at the screen door, sniffing wistfully at a fine new round of golden cheese. Bill Burg tossed the animal a sliver of rind, and the hound trotted away, leaving mute thanks and a faint odor of vanquished polecats.

The next comer was a buyer, a farmer well dressed and self-assured. He wanted a plowshare, three sizes of hemp rope, a horse collar, some canned goods, a new lamp, a pair of overalls, some work shoes, an outlay of gingham for his wife's new dresses, and a bottle of pasteurized milk for the baby. He had brought along seven dozen eggs, three gallons of sorghum molasses, and six pounds of fresh pork sausage as part payment. Bill Burg completed the deal with friendliness and ease, and rang up the cash and barter total on his register.

Country trade rests basically on a sound commodity dollar—not a credit or a speculation dollar. It is based upon tangibles.

The crossroads store revels in its chance for directness, intimacy of merchant and customer, close understanding of regular and seasonal needs of a given farm community. Proprietors are apt to be home folks, bred to the ways and views of their communities. They are justified, too, in carrying a surprisingly large range of goods. Rents and building overhead stand at a minimum.

And there's the staple advantage of barter trade. Bill Burg does about 40 percent of his trade in barter. He takes herbs, ginseng, poultry, eggs, cream, cured meats, butter, berries, fruits, grains, potatoes, any saleable produce in exchange for store goods, which makes possible a double profit to him. Both profits can be whittled to a minimum and still leave a chance for staying in business.

Then the crossroads store holds an advantage in natural history. Vast numbers of farm communities still require a home trading center. Fine highways and cheap autos have taken much of the time and labor out of going to market, but as yet they haven't succeeded in doing away with the expense thereof.

The country storekeeper has various possibilities in side lines. He may take on such side jobs as leather mending, milk testing, egg candling, tire repairing, and auto service. Like some 47,000 other crossroads merchants, Bill Burg keeps a post office in connection with his store, which gathers in trade and so gives reasonable pay for time and trouble. Like many another, he also runs a farm. In emergencies, Bill Burg still has the heft to do considerable good as a blacksmith. Back in his younger days, he rigged up a barber chair and turned tonsorial artist on Saturday afternoons. Now he has abandoned that enterprise, but his barber chair still waits back in the storage room, a throne amid the assemblage of harnesses, wagon parts, and light farm machinery.

Finally, the crossroads store has a first cut of the invaluable resource of countryside friendship, a handy gathering place for spending an off afternoon or a rainy day, a place where farm folks may gather for checkers or horseshoes, or to trade ideas on crops and farming ways and each other.

The country storekeeper is not merely a business man. It has been Bill Burg's pleasure, and otherwise, to make arrangements for weddings, funerals, christenings, church revivals, family reunions, and neighborhood fun-makings. He has set broken arms, dug beans out of little boys' noses, washed and bandaged wounds, witnessed wills and contracts.

In fact, his weathered little store has been the scene of both weddings and births. Bill Burg has stopped runaways, risked a years' supply of victuals to a lank and hungry farm boy who is now an eminent United States senator, gone far out of his way to deliver telegrams and messages of great sorrow or joy. But he figures all this is part of the job of the crossroads store and its keeper. He has never yet taken a penny's pay for a favor.

Trouble? Sure. But it's not always a loss. For instance, about forty years ago, a little girl came in this store with a pair of worn-out shoes. She wanted new buttons sewed on 'em. I always did that free. But I saw those shoes were leaking water. They needed soles worse than buttons. It was a deadish kind of day, cold and murky, and not having much else to do, after I'd sewed on the buttons I put on a new pair of half soles—also free.

Well, that little girl has been pretty fond of me ever since. She's my wife now, and the best investment I ever made or hope to make.

Yessir, and a free favor was my next best investment. Sam Carter came into these parts about 1910. Sam's a mighty good citizen, but at the start he and I didn't hit it off so well. For one thing, I'm a Democrat and Sam's a Republican. And Sam's a fiend for accuracy. Unluckily, on the first good order he bought here, I got mixed up on the sizing of some plow parts and caused him considerable delay and trouble. So he decided I was a stick-in-the-mud, and I sized him up as something of a crank. That went on for quite a spell.

Then Sam's little boy took diphtheria. Sam had to come to my store to phone for a doctor. The doctor had to get some antidiphtheria toxin, which was rare back in those days. I helped him wire for it. But somehow or other the drug company sent the serum to me instead of to Sam. Well, Sam didn't have a phone, of course, and he lived about nine miles off in one of the roughest hollers you ever laid eyes on.

But I knew it was a life or death business, so I shut store, hopped on my horse, and delivered the medicine. Sam was pacing about like a locoed horse, and when I got there the doctor gave me a bear-hug and told me I'd saved the boy's life. When Sam tried to pay me, I told him I only sold merchandise.

After that, Sam got to be my customer. And he's what the town folks call an agricultural genius. He's built up the finest dairy and fruit farms in this neck of the woods, and his trade alone averages a third of my total business. He's still a Republican, but he's the best customer I ever had, and next to my wife, about the best friend.

A farm wife, in checkered gingham and broad straw hat, came marketing, with six red hens waiting outside, in a crate, duly shaded from the summer sun. A clattering of heavy steps foretold the arrival of new trade. I reveled in the fact that the crossroads store remains an exchange center for ideas and companionships, as well as for goods and dollars; that through its doors pass the whole scope of rural humanity, young and old, poor and prosperous. Old-timers gather to relive lost youth through talk. Farm wives, come for a turn of store-shopping, look serenely upon a world they no longer have cause to fear. There are yearning maidens, sunburnt scholars, fuzzy-faced farm youths come to watch the ways of trade, little girls with classic names and sunbrowned legs, come for penny candy bags, and perhaps to listen to the words of great and knowing men.

The countryside generally is free to congregate on shady steps or porch benches or sturdy counters, or to encircle patriarchal monkey-stoves as weather decides, there to think and speak upon people, politics, hopes, jokes, and allegiances, lost, found, and otherwise. As a rule these store-porch Americans are good listeners and keen observers. They laugh a great deal, revel in simple drolleries such as that of the countryside dim-wit who propounds the problem that if two black snakes, each one thirty inches long, met up together and started swallowing each other at the rate of an inch a minute, then at the end of thirty minutes, what would there be left?

LAW MAKERS AND BREAKERS [2]

To say that peasant Americans are prevailingly ignorant of law would be a long way from accuracy. Granting that law exercises a convenient minimum of influence upon backwoods morality, the run of upbrush citizenry are surprisingly well informed upon legal procedure and are deft enough when it comes to courtroom craftiness. The chances are that virtually any hill-billy or rural commoner of legal age will understand the how of avoiding a jury summons, how to turn state's evidence, how to frustrate an embarrassing cross-examination, or how to entangle a too inquiring judge. Accordingly the great majority of rural court records reveal a decidedly low ratio of conviction.

Courts, old and new, frontier and modern, backwoods and city, have always been homes of contention, cases for argument and ethical indecision, havens for talk and ponder.

Much of the old survives in our contemporary backwoods courts. Circuit sittings in April and November are still gala events of many an isolated countryside, replete with the picnicking spirit of an invincible frontier. Country people still come by the festive wagonload to hear the court "set" and the lawyers "plead." Blue-denimed farmers come to wait out a change in the weather. Farm wives come along for surcease of confining kitchens. There are school youngsters and upcountry damsels come upon with restless yearnings, and funny-faced farm boys, out to look and listen, and to learn the ways of town and of success. So the courtroom

[2] From *Backwoods America*, by Charles Morrow Wilson, journalist and specialist on rural America. University of North Carolina Press. '34. Excerpts from p 133–72. Reprinted by permission of the author.

becomes the most colorful and homely of human documents. Jurors, judges, sheriffs, deputies and barristers, and spectators keep to their established places only until matters come to be dramatic; then all of them come to be a common and closely pressed multitude, who look generally alike, sit alike, smell alike.

Neither principals nor spectators appear to be distressed by the closeness or cumbersomeness of legal procedures. They are a slow people in a slow country. Cases range from the picturesquely trivial to the conventionally sordid. Among criminal cases, moonshining charges were probably the most common in old court days, as they are in the backwoods courts of today. Moonshining is approximately as old as are isolated peoples and, from all appearances, about as hard to do away with. Next to moonshining in number of cases come killings. Too much liquor, a game of horseshoes, or a family row are the bases for a majority of the shootings and knifings of today, just as they were a century ago, for in our contemporary back hills much of the spirit of the frontier endures. . . .

The old-style rural Justice of Peace courts represent other warming chapters in humbler realms of jurisprudence.

So far as I am able to gather, the nation's dizziest J.P. trial took place underneath a sycamore tree on the bank of Leatherneck Creek in Madison County, Arkansas.

A countryman had been accused of stealing a hog. The trial lasted three days and required half a hundred witnesses and twice as many arguments.

The court had but one law book, that a copy of the Illinois Statutes of ancient vintage. The judge's bench was a whiskey barrel, full, upon which the court sat a-straddle. At recurring interludes he would declare a recess and sell whiskey to the jury, defendant, witnesses, and spectators, and to himself. The liquor was sold on credit, with names and amounts chalked up on the sides of the barrel.

By the end of three days several developments had materialized. Three of the jury had fallen into the creek and four more were effectively passed out. The Justice, himself exceedingly drunk, finally dismissed the case on the grounds that the jury was incompetent to try it. . . .

In another case, after listening to the testimony and argument for both sides, the old Justice wiped his mustache and announced:

If I was to believe all the defence has said, I'd turn the defendant loose, and if I believed all the prosecution says I'd send him to jail for life. But gentlemen, if things was jest as they be, and I don't believe a damn word neither of 'em says, I don't know what the hell I'm gonna do.

They's been moonshinin' in these parts since earliest pioneerin' days, and I wouldn't be none surprised but what they always will be. We ain't got no call to be ashamed of ourselves, nor of anything we do. Moonshinin's a man's game. Can't jest any punkin-roller stick it.

Uncle Dick Saulee is in no manner a bootlegger. He and his boy Alfred have built up a far-reaching reputation for good quality whiskey and the trade comes to their door. They are exclusive in their choice of patrons. They observe the finer ethics of the trade and they testify with a considerable lift of pride that the majority of old-time moonshiners are a rather high caliber of men, scions of strong pioneer families, of old settlers lost among old hills.

The run of old-school moonshiners do not object to the enforcement of order and honesty. The young roughnecks who stay drunk on their own wares and crave trouble must, of course, be attended to, and no reasonable-minded citizen can deny that. But the experienced backwoods sheriff usually looks with leniency upon the old-hand operator who can make good whiskey and behave himself while about it.

Taking them generally, the old-timers are men of moderate habit. Occasionally one degenerates into a year-round sot, but such instances are exceptional. In matters aside from liquor making, the profession has kept traditionally to the side of the law and order. Study the court dockets and you will find that very few moonshiners have ever been up for larceny and banditry. In the horse-thieving days of Arkansas, Missouri, and Tennessee, moonshiners were point-blank enemies of the rustlers. Again, back in the early eighties, when much of the southern hill country was infested with an organization of upbrush kluxers known as Bald Knobbers, the moonshiners stood squarely against them. And although the Knobbers took in after the shiners with all the pious zeal of thirty-seven Israelites after a Hittite, the Bald Knobbers have come to be only a people of fireside legendry, whereas the moonshiners continue to flourish as they probably always will.

Uncle Dick Saulee is no harsh critic of the law. He believes that the run of county sheriffs are square-dealing men, braver and more sporting than the run of federal men. The older Saulee had several points of objection to federal prohibition enforcement, the most flagrant being the use of undercover men.

When county officials fail to fill the court dockets with indictments as they are wont nowadays to do, then the powers of prohibition enforcement are prone to resort to stool pigeons. One such case came up to War Eagle country not many months ago, representing himself as an old-time shiner from Kentucky, honin' after new trade and new territory. He set beer, equipped a still, made and sold liquor. He made friends with the countryside moonshiners, traded recipes and worms and mash vats and kettles. He partook of their open-hearted hospitality and indulged in Saturday night socials.

Then one day the newcomer packed up and left. But on his way out he stopped at the county seat and turned in warrants for every moonshiner up the creek bottom. And word leaked out that the informant was a prohibitioner—an officer but certainly no gentleman.

Uncle Dick admits straightforwardly that he doesn't fancy that sort of doings. Apparently the forces of justice didn't either. For the grand jury failed to return an indictment in all twenty-two of the cases.

Virtually any upbrush countryside abounds with instances of legalized cussedness. There are phony raiding parties and minions of law who shoot without discretion or sobriety, and deaths result. Federal enforcement luminaries come down into the hills honing after raidings and gunplay, and then the county officials are put to their mettle to avoid needless bloodshed and at the same time to bolster the dignity of the law.

Once a party of federal men came down to an Arkansas village, called on the sheriff and demanded that he lead them on a raid up War Eagle Creek. The sheriff complied, and in the course of searching the raiders passed within an easy stone's throw of Uncle Dick's location and trampled squarely over a bed of his buried whiskey. The Saulees had buried a run for curing and planted over the place with blackberry briars.

Next day while strolling, Alfred passed the place, picked up the sheriff's wallet, which was empty save for a scribbled note:

"Dick, them blackberry bushes don't look quite natural enough. No harm done yet, though. These yahoos couldn't tell a blackberry from a pawpaw."

Alfred returned the wallet.

Laying aside all personal interests and enterprises, Uncle Dick protests against legislation that would condemn to prison an old farm wife who might squeeze out a cup of blackberry cordial for tonicking a teething child, or a commoner who would transport a sip of elderberry wine to a fellow who lies in sickness and suffering. He revels in the fact that the mad era of fanaticism known as Volsteadism is finished.

The old-style making of moonshine is hard and laborious. To begin with, the starch of the corn must be converted into sugar. Some distillers accomplish this metamorphosis in a few hours with the use of yeast and barley malt. But most of the old-timers are sot against such artifices. Instead, they prefer to shell the corn into a vessel with a vent in its bottom; then they pour hot water over the top of the container. As the water percolates out of the vent, more is poured on, and this is kept up for several days until the corn grains have sprouted. The diastase in the germinating seed produces the same chemical effect as malt.

Then the sprouted corn is dried and ground into very coarse meal. This "sweet meal" is converted into a mash by the adding of boiling water, and after standing a few days, the decoction is broken up and poured over with sugar, preferably corn sugar, and water. Fermentation takes from four to ten days. During the whole of this period the mash must be kept at precisely the right temperature. Too much heat spoils the body of the whiskey, and too little will kill fermentation. That is another good reason why a moonshiner must have both diligence and skill, for the chances are that his fingers must serve as thermometer and his tongue as saccharometer.

So the sweet mash becomes sour mash, and in the changing the sugar becomes alcohol and carbonic acid. The resulting liquid is commonly known as "beer," occasionally as "wash." It is intoxicating, but sour and puckery as a green persimmon. The test for final completion requires that one put an ear to the bottom of the container. If it sounds like "rain on a tin roof," then the batch is ready to be worked.

The "beer" is poured into the tank of the still, a vessel with a closed head connected with a "worm," a spiral copper tube, surrounded by a jacket, through which cool water is kept passing. A fire is built in the still furnace and slow boiling begins. Spirit vapors and steam are condensed during the course of their passage through the worm, and so trickle down into the receiving jug. The first comings are called "low wines" or "singlings." They are weak in alcohol and strong in fusels and other rank oils. Accordingly the painstaking moonshiner must re-distill his "low wines" at a diminished temperature.

The liquor of second distillation is called "doublings." If underdistilled, the doublings will be rank and weak; if overdistilled, almost pure alcohol. Old-style moonshiners make their final test by reckoning the "bead" of the liquor, estimating the how of the little iridescent bubbles which rise to the surface when the bottle is tilted. If the bubbles rise and stay put, the shiner will vouch for the product; if not, he will pass it by, regardless of label or testimony.

Finally the liquor is run through a charcoal filter. The result is moonshine in the raw, a fluid limpid as water, and almost as colorless. It has a faint smoky aroma, and feels raw and fiery to the palate. As a beverage it is unique, as an intoxicant a profound success.

Most moonshiners prefer to operate along small creeks, with banks closely choked with bushes and briars. Sometimes the locations have primitive fortifications, such as brush pitfalls or barricades of logs. Sometimes entanglements of wire are stretched among surrounding trees to make impossible a quick charge through them.

The still is usually covered with a shed, built low, so that it may be well screened by the surrounding underbrush. Behind the still shed, far enough to be in deep shadows, even when the furnace is going, there is likely to be a pallet for the night watch or alternate firemen. As a general proposition, the fire must be kept burning continuously for from sixty to seventy-five hours.

Moonshiners are troubled with any number of incidental aggravants. Most operating areas are in open-range country. Cattle are attracted by the odors of distilling and hogs are passionately fond of still slops and "beers." They can likely scent them and trail down their source for half a dozen cross-country miles. Horses have a high tension loathing for moonshine, and for that reason they can be used very effectively for locating stills. I have heard stories of an old-school revenue officer who used to ride through the rough country on horseback. Whenever he came to a creek or a river ford he gave his mount renewed opportunity for sampling the water. If the water bore even the faintest flavor of still slop, the horse would shake his head violently and refuse to drink. Then the cue was to follow up the stream bed and so to locate the still.

Uncle Dick Saulee estimates that at the present time the actual production cost of moonshine is about two dollars a gallon. He has kept accurate accounts for the past nine years. Here is his table of production cost for one gallon of double-distilled whiskey:

One-half bushel of corn	$ .30
Six pounds corn sugar	.36
Malt, rye, yeast, and incidentals	.12
Milling costs	.10
Labor, reckoned at 25 cents an hour	.37
Still, equipment, and transportation of ingredients	.12
Firewood	.08
Oak kegs for seasoning, jars, jugs, etc.	.22
	$1.67

The days of high profits are generally dead. Even moonshining must at least approximate a competitive level. The three or four years which followed the enactment of the Volstead Act were a low era of whiskey-making—they were an era of highjackers, fly-by-nights, botched brews and weird and unholy substitutes. The fine old profession of moonshining was threatened with inglorious oblivion. Illicit liquor then brought unheard of prices—twenty and even forty dollars a gallon. There were court instances of two gallons of whiskey having been made from one bushel of corn and sold at forty dollars a gallon. A gallon of respectable moonshine was made to do service for two or three gallons by diluting it with water and adding lye or tobacco juice to give a bite and washing powder to provide the bead. This recipe was actually entered as court testimony in an important Carolina moonshining trial:

One bushel of corn meal, one hundred pounds of sugar, two three-pound cans of lye, four pounds of ripe poke berries, two of baking soda. Water to measure and distill. The decoction was reckoned to make fourteen gallons.

Moonshining still holds its peculiar economic vantage in the far hinterlands, particularly of the South. Most moonshining areas are, at least agriculturally speaking, sections of increasing poverty. Hillside fields are quick to lose their fertility. Hard wood timber is quickly exhausted and slow to replace itself. As a usual proposition the hill-country farmer draws the worst of the economic servings. Roads are poor, transportation is expensive and damaging, cooperative methods are unused, and legitimate markets hover perpetually at a low ebb.

So the hill-country homesteader must plant with a basic idea of self-sufficiency, and too often depend upon cash-bringing sidelines to equip himself and family with an occasional change of clothes and winter shoes. In the run of instances the old-style moonshiner continues to grow his corn, to haul it to mill, to look after its grinding, to set the brew, to attend to testing and firing. He buries the cache for curing and stands all risk for its distribution. The procedure is old and long established. Likely his father did the same before him, and his grandfather, and his great-grandfather. Statute laws grow yellow and musty with age and disuse, but the mandates of primitive economy, although a thousand times older than man-made laws, keep always a virile youthfulness, an unquenchable power.

The practice of advertising usually creeps into the industry only at the outer fringes. The true-blue hill-country moonshiner makes and sells, and reckons personal integrity and artisan standards to serve as advertising. He is possessed of a keen critical reckoning and he presupposes that the customer understands wares and their degree of excellence.

But if the prospective buyer does not, then the chances are that the moonshiner will qualify with a candidness that is, in these days of synthetic flavors and faked labels, nothing short of astonishing.

We once went out into the Arkansas hills in quest of a smooth and dependable brandy for the balm and unction of an elderly gentleman who was convalescing from a bad siege of sickness. We dropped by Sol Muster's place out among the tater-knob hills about Weddington Gap. We explained our mission and desires.

Mr. Muster scratched his white head with a remaining stub of hand:

"Well, I make brandy,—shore. And all considered hit's purty fair drinkin' licker . . . and if you-all wanted hit for your own pussonal use, I wouldn't have no back-drawin's about sellin' hit to you, because you-all is well and walkin'. . . . But an old gent that's been ailin'—I just don't believe he'd ought to drink this here brandy a-tall."

As far as the moonshiner is concerned, high pressure salesmanship is out of his rightful field. That is relegated to the distributor who takes liquor out of the hill country down to valley towns. These entrepreneurs have sundry advertising ways. Among the most picturesque of them is the open distribution of moonshine samples at conventions or county fairs or rallies or picnics, or the still more novel institution of the sampling house station—an open house, well stocked and conveniently located, where prospective purchasers may come to taste before they buy.

Inside such a place one is welcomed with easy chairs and open kegs and cooling chasers and diplomatic sales talks. Then after two or three swigs of third-rate nectar the prospect will find himself recipient of tactfully timed discourses on the obvious quality and the excelling skill of the maker. Then one staggers forth to recite to his townsmen the marvels of his findings. And so the word is spread.

We were asking Dick Saulee about the probable outcome of a stranger's blundering upon a still in active operation.

"Well, they'd likely ask you some questions about who you was an what you was doin' in that neck of the woods. Then if what you said sounded all right they'd likely get you to do some trifling work about the still—so to make you one of them in the sight of the law. . . . Of course they could tell considerable about you without asking. . . . They wouldn't gain nothin' by damagin' you, besides, moonshiners ain't generally vicious. And people is jest bound to know a mighty lot about moonshiners, nohow."

By way of illustrating the point he told of a confederate named Lige Yeater. Lige recently left Arkansas in order to better liquor conditions in Oregon. When he got ready to leave, he started the word about that on a given date he reckoned to hold an auction sale for the purpose of disposing of all his distilling equipment and his surplus of liquor. The sale was duly attended by more than four hundred people, among them moonshiners from all over the Ozarks, dealers from neighboring cities, townsmen of all grades, a sheriff, a mayor, two judges and six doctors, and two representatives of the press. Two stills and six hundred gallons of liquor were auctioned, refreshments were served on the ground, and a good time was had by all.

WHEN THE FARMS BLEW AWAY [3]

It was on Armistice Day of 1933 that the first of the great dust storms swept across South Dakota.

By mid-morning a gale was blowing, cold and black. By noon it was blacker than night, because one can see through night and this was an opaque black. It was a wall of dirt one's eyes could not penetrate, but it could penetrate the eyes and ears and nose. It could penetrate to the lungs until one coughed up black. If a person was outside, he tied his handkerchief around his face, but he still coughed up black; and inside the house the Karnstrums soaked sheets and towels and stuffed them around the window ledges, but these didn't help much.

They were afraid, because they had never seen anything like this before. . . .

When the wind died and the sun shown forth again, it was on a different world. There were no fields, only sand drifting into mounds and eddies that swirled in what was now but an autumn breeze. There was no longer a section-line road fifty feet from the

[3] Excerpt from *Since Yesterday*, by Frederick Lewis Allen, American social historian. Harper. '39. p 196–214. Copyright 1939, 1940 by Harper & Row, Publishers, Inc; renewed 1967, 1968 by Agnes R. Allen. Reprinted by permission of the publisher.

front door. It was obliterated. In the farmyard, fences, machinery, and trees were gone, buried. The roofs of sheds stuck out through drifts deeper than a man is tall.

I quote from an account by R. D. Lusk, in the *Saturday Evening Post* [August 13, 1938], of the way in which that first great storm of blowing dust hit the 470-acre Karnstrum farm in Beadle County, South Dakota. But the description might apply equally well to thousands of other farms on the Great Plains all the way from the Texas Panhandle up to the Canadian border, and to any one of numberless storms that swept the Plains during the next two years. For the "great black blizzard" of November 11, 1933—which darkened the sky in Chicago the following day and as far east as Albany, New York, the day after that—was only a prelude to disaster. During 1934 and 1935 thousands of square miles were to be laid waste and their inhabitants set adrift upon desperate migrations across the land.

Long afterward, an elderly farm woman from the Dust Bowl—one of that straggling army of refugees whose predicament has been made vivid to hundreds of thousands of readers in Steinbeck's *The Grapes of Wrath*—told her story to Paul Taylor and Dorothea Lange in California. She described how her family had done pretty well on their Arkansas farm until the Depression, when prices had fallen and they had found themselves in hard straits. "And then," said she, "the Lord taken a hand."

To many others it must have seemed as if the Lord had taken a hand in bringing the dust storms: as if, not content with visiting upon the country a man-made crisis—a Depression caused by men's inability to manage their economic affairs farsightedly—an omnipotent power had followed it with a visitation of nature: the very land itself had risen in revolt. (To other people, omnipotence may have seemed to be enjoying a sardonic joke at the expense of the New Deal's Agricultural Adjustment program: "So it's crop-reduction you want, is it? Well, I'll show you.") Yet this was no blind stroke of nature such as that of the hurricane which, wandering far from the paths usually followed by hurricanes, tore across New England in the fall of 1938, swamping towns, ripping up forests, and taking nearly seven hundred lives. There was a long story of human error behind it.

During the latter part of the nineteenth century the Great Plains—a region of light rainfall, of sun and high winds, of waving grasses, "where seldom is heard a discouraging word, and the skies are not cloudy all day"—had been the great cattle country of the nation: a vast open area, unfenced at first, where the cowboys tended the cattle-kings' herds. Before the end of the century this range had been badly damaged by overgrazing, according to contemporary federal reports, and the land was being heavily invaded by homesteaders, who tried manfully to wring a living from the semi-arid soil. But it was not until the Great War brought a huge demand for wheat, and tractors for large-scale machine farming became available, that the Plains began to come into their own as a crop-producing country, and the sod-covering which had protected them was plowed up on the grand scale. Throughout the 1920s the area devoted to big wheat farms expanded. A new power era had come, it was said, to revolutionize American agriculture; factory methods were being triumphantly applied to the land.

To be sure, there wasn't much rain. The mean annual rainfall was only between 10 and 20 inches on the Plains (as compared with, for example, 20 to 40 in the Mississippi Valley region, 40 to 50 in the North Atlantic region, 40 to 60 in the Ohio and Tennessee basins, and 75 and more in the Pacific Northwest). But there was a pretty favorable series of years during the 1920s and the farmers were not much disturbed.

In a recent report of the National Resources Committee there is a revealing map. It shows—by means of black dots scattered over the United States—the regions where there was an increase, between 1919 and 1929, in the acreage of land in harvested crops: in short, it shows the regions newly invaded by the crop farmer. Easily the most conspicuous feature of the map is an irregular blur of those black dots running from north to south just a little east of the Rocky Mountains—running from the Canadian border at the northern edge of Montana and North Dakota, down through the Dakotas, western Kansas and Nebraska and eastern Colorado, and then into Oklahoma and northern Texas. This, very roughly, was the next region of promise—and the region of future tragedy.

Nineteen-thirty was a bad year in parts of this territory—and worse elsewhere; it was then, you may recall, that President Hoover was agitated over the question whether federal money should be granted to drought-distressed farmers. Nineteen-thirty-one was worse in the Dakotas; 1932 was better. Then came 1933: it was a swinger, hot and dry. During that first summer of the New Deal, farmers in South Dakota were finding that they couldn't raise even enough corn to feed the livestock. In western Kansas not a drop of rain fell for months. Already the topsoil was blowing; there were places in Kansas where it was said that farmers had to excavate their tractors before they could begin to plow. That fall came the Armistice Day black blizzard.

But it was during 1934 and 1935—the years when Roosevelt was pushing through his financial reforms, and Huey Long was a national portent, and the languishing NRA [National Recovery Act] was put out of its misery by the Supreme Court—that the thermometer in Kansas stayed week after week at 108 or above and the black storms raged again and again. The drought continued acute during much of 1936. Oklahoma farms became great dunes of shifting sand (so like seashore dunes, said one observer, that one almost expected to smell the salt). Housewives in the drought belt kept oiled cloths on the window sills and between the upper and lower sashes of the windows, and some of them tried to seal up every aperture in their houses with the gummed paper strips used in wrapping parcels, yet still the choking dust filtered in and lay in ripples on the kitchen floor, while outside it blew blindingly across a No Man's Land; roads and farm buildings and once green thickets half-buried in the sand. It was in those days that a farmer, sitting at his window during a dust storm, remarked that he was counting the Kansas farms as they came by.

Retribution for the very human error of breaking the sod of the Plains had come in full measure. And, as often happens, it was visited upon the innocent as well as upon the guilty—if indeed one could single out any individuals as guilty of so pervasive an error as social shortsightedness.

Westward Flight

Westward fled the refugees from this new Sahara, as if obedient to the old American tradition that westward lies the land of promise. In 1934 and 1935 Californians became aware of an increasing influx into their state of families and groups of families of "Okies," traveling in ancient family jalopies; but for years the streams of humanity continued to run. They came along US Highway 30 through the Idaho hills, along Highway 66 across New Mexico and Arizona, along the Old Spanish Trail through El Paso, along all the other westward trails. They came in decrepit, square-shouldered 1925 Dodges and 1927 La Salles; in battered 1923 Model-T Fords that looked like relics of some antique culture; in trucks piled high with mattresses and cooking utensils and children, with suitcases, jugs, and sacks strapped to the running boards. "They roll westward like a parade," wrote Richard L. Neuberger [journalist and legislator. *Our Promised Land*. Macmillan. 1938]. "In a single hour from a grassy meadow near an Idaho road I counted thirty-four automobiles with the license plates of states between Chicago and the mountains."

They left behind them a half-depopulated countryside. A survey of the farmhouses in seven counties of southeastern Colorado, made in 1936, showed 2,878 houses still occupied, 2,811 abandoned; and there were also, in that area, 1,522 abandoned homesites. The total number of drought refugees who took the westward trek over the mountains was variously estimated in 1939 at from 200,000 upwards—with more coming all the time.

As these wanderers moved along the highways they became a part of a vast and confused migratory movement. When they camped by the wayside they might find themselves next to a family of evicted white Alabama sharecroppers who had been on the move for four years, snatching seasonal farm-labor jobs wherever they could through the Southwest; or next to tenant families from Arkansas Delta who had been "tractored off" their land—expelled in order that the owner might consolidate two or three farms and operate them with tractors and day labor; or next to lone wanderers who had once held industrial jobs and had now for years been on relief or on the road—jumping freights, hitchhiking, panhandling, shunting back and forth across the countryside in the faint hope of a durable job. And when these varied streams of migrants reached the Coast they found themselves in desperate competition for jobs with individuals or families who for years had been "fruit tramps," moving northward each year with the harvests from the Imperial Valley in southern California to the Sacramento Valley or even to the apple-picking in the Yakima Valley in Washington.

Here in the land of promise, agriculture had long been partly industrialized. Huge farms were in the control of absentee owners or banks or corporations, and were accustomed to depend upon the labor of migratory "fruit tramps" who had formerly been mostly Mexicans, Japanese, and other foreigners, but now were increasingly Americans. Those laborers who were lucky enough to get jobs picking cotton or peas or fruit would be sheltered temporarily in camps consisting typically of frame cabins in rows, with a water line between every two rows; they were very likely to find in their cabin no stove, no cots, no water pail. Even the best of the camps offered a way of life strikingly different from that of the ruggedly individualist farmer of the American tradition, who owned his farm or else was preparing, by working as a resident "hired man," or by renting a farm, for the chance of ultimate ownership. These pickers were homeless, voteless nomads, unwanted anywhere save at the harvest season.

When wave after wave of the new migrants reached California, the labor market became glutted, earnings were low, and jobs became so scarce that groups of poverty-stricken families would be found squatting in makeshift Hoovervilles or bunking miserably in their awkward old Fords by the roadside. Being Americans of native stock and accustomed to independence, they took the meager wages and the humiliation bitterly, sought to organize, talked of striking, sometimes struck. At every such threat, something like panic seized the growers. If this new proletariat were permitted to organize, and were to strike at picking time, they might ruin the whole season's output of a perishable crop. There followed antipicketing ordinances; the spectacle of armed deputies dislodging the migrants from their pitiful camps; violence by bands of vigilantes, to whom these ragged families were not fellow-citizens who had suffered in a great American disaster but dirty, ignorant, superstitious outlanders, failures at life, easy dupes for "red" agitators. This engulfing tide of discontent must be kept moving.

Farther north the refugees were likely to be received with more sympathy, especially in regions where the farms were small and not industrialized; here and there one heard of instances of real hospitality, such as that of the Oregon town which held a canning festival for the benefit of the drought victims in the neighborhood. The well-managed camps set up by the Farm Security Administration were havens of human decency. But to the vast majority of the refugees the promised land proved to be a place of new and cruel tragedy.

Farm Tenancy and Farm Industrialism

These unhappy wanderers of the West were only a small minority of the farmers of the United States. What was happening to the rest of them?

We have already seen the AAA [Agricultural Adjustment Administration] beginning the colossal task of making acreage-reduction agreements with millions of farmers in the hope of jacking up the prices of crops and thus restoring American agriculture to economic health. We have seen it making credit available to farmers and trying, through the Farm Mortgage Moratorium Act and other legislation, to free them of the immediate hazards of debt. Just how successful the AAA program could be considered was still, at the end of the decade,* a subject of ferocious controversy, if only because one could not separate its effect upon prices from the effects wrought by the drought and by the general improvement in economic conditions after 1933. But certainly farm prices rose. For example, the farmer who had received, on the average, only 33 cents a bushel for wheat in 1933 received 69 cents in 1934, 89 cents in 1935, 92 cents in 1936, $1.24 in 1937, and 88 cents in 1938. The cotton farmer who had received an average price of 5.6 cents a pound for his cotton in 1933 received between 10 and 13 cents during the next four years, and 7.9 cents in 1938. And certainly there was a general improvement in the condition of those farmers who owned their own farms—and lived outside the worst drought areas. A survey of three thousand farms in various parts of the country—mostly better-than-average farms—made by the Department of Agriculture in 1938 showed a distinct gain in equipment and in comfort; more of these farms had electricity than in 1930, more had tractors and trucks, more had bathrooms, automobiles, and radios. But this was not a complete picture of what had happened.

To begin with, quantities of farmers had lost their farms during the hideous early years of the Depression—lost them by reason of debt. These farms had mostly fallen into the hands of banks or insurance companies, or of small-town investors who had held the mortgages on them, or were being held by government bodies for nonpayment of taxes, or had been bought in at tax sales. As early as 1934, the National Resources Board stated that nearly 30 percent of the total value of farm land in the West North Central States was owned by "creditor or government agencies which have been compelled to take over the property." At the small prairie city, the local representative of a big New York insurance company was a very busy man, supervising the management of tracts of property far and wide. The tentacles of the octopus of metropolitan financial control reached more deeply than ever before into the prairie country—though one must add that this octopus was a most unwilling one, and would have been only too glad to let go if it could only get its money back. (As time went on, the Metropolitan and other insurance companies made determined efforts to find buyers for their farm properties, financing these buyers on easy terms.) In the callous old Wall Street phrase, the farms of the United States had been "passing into stronger hands"; and that meant that more and more of them, owned by people who did not live on them, were being operated by tenants.

For over half a century at least, farm tenancy had been on the increase in the United States. Back in 1880, only 25 percent of American farms had been run by tenants. Slowly the percentage had increased; now, during the Depression, it reached 42. The growth of tenantry caused many misgivings, for not only did it shame the fine old Jeffersonian ideal of individual landholding—an ideal in which most Americans firmly believed—but it had other disadvantages. Tenants were not likely to put down roots, did not feel a full sense of responsibility for the land and equipment they used, were likely to let it deteriorate, and in general were less substantial citizens than those farmers who had a permanent share in the community. In 1935, less than two thirds of the tenant farmers in the United States had occupied their present land for more than one year! In the words of Charles and Mary Beard [*America in Midpassage*. Macmillan. 1939],

Tenants wandered from farm to farm, from landlord to landlord, from region to region, on foot, in battered wagons, or in dilapidated automobiles, commonly dragging families with them, usually to conditions lower in the scale of living than those from which they had fled.

The passing of farms into "stronger hands" was accompanied by another change. More and more the farm owner, whether or not he operated his own farm, was coming to think of himself as a business man, to think of farming as a business. He was less likely to use his farm as a means of subsistence, more likely to use as much of it as possible for the growing of crops for sale. He was more interested in bookkeeping, more alert to the advantages of farm machinery, and especially of operating with tractors on the largest possible scale. A striking example of this trend was the appearance of the "suitcase farmer"—a small-town business man who bought a farm or two, cleared them of houses and barns, spent a few weeks of each year planting and harvesting them (using his own tractor or a hired one), and otherwise devoted himself to his business, not living on the land at all. A Kansas banker . . . toward the end of the decade . . . estimated that between 20 and 30 percent of the land in western Kansas was owned by suitcase farmers. This was what was happening to the territory whence the victims of drought had fled!

In certain parts of the South and Southwest this trend toward making a mechanized business of farming took a form even more sinister in the eyes of those who believed in the Jeffersonian tradition. In these districts farm tenancy was becoming merely a way station on the road to farm industrialism. The tenants themselves were being eliminated. Furthermore, the AAA, strangely enough, was unwittingly assisting the process.

How easy for an owner of farm property, when the government offered him a check for reducing his acreage in production, to throw out some of his tenants or sharecroppers, buy a tractor with the check, and run his farm mechanically with the aid of hired labor—not the sort of year-round hired labor which the old-time "hired man" had represented, but labor engaged only by the day when there happened to be work to be done! During the 1930s large numbers of renters and sharecroppers, both black and white, were being displaced in the South—to the tune of angry protests by the Southern Tenant Farmers' Union, equally angry retaliation by the landlords and their allies, and a deal of the sort of barbarous cruelty which we have noted in California. In the areas where large-scale cotton farming with the aid of machinery was practicable, tenants were expelled right and left. *Fortune* told of a big Mississippi planter who bought twenty-two tractors and thirteen 4-row cultivators, evicted no less than 130 of his 160 sharecropper families, and kept only 30 for day laborers. During the years 1930–1937, the sales of farm tractors in ten cotton states increased no less than 90 percent—and the indications were that at the end of that period the increase was accelerating. While the number of farms operated by tenants was growing elsewhere in the country between 1930 and 1935, it actually declined a little in the West South Central States. In two cotton counties of the Texas Panhandle, studied by Paul S. Taylor in 1937, it declined sharply. And here was the reason:

Commonly, the landlord who purchases a tractor throws two 160-acre farms operated by tenants into an operating unit, and lets both tenants go. Sometimes the rate of displacement is greater, rising to 8, 10, and even 15 families of tenants.

Where did the displaced tenants go? Into the towns, some of them. In many rural areas, census figures showed an increased town population and simultaneously a depopulated countryside. Said the man at a gas station in a Texas town, "This relief is ruining the town. They come in from the country to get on relief." Some of them got jobs running tractors on other farms at $1.25 a day. Some went on to California: out of farming as a settled way of life into farming as big business dependent on a large, mobile supply of labor.

So far this new pattern was only fragmentary and was confined mostly to the South and West, though the number of migratory farm workers was growing fast even along the Atlantic seaboard. [See *The Way of the Farmer*, below in this section.] Perhaps the onrushing agricultural industrialism would prove as short-lived as the earlier epidemic of tractor farming which had promised so much for the Great Plains during the 1920s—would lead once more to depletion of the soil and thus to its own undoing as well as the land's. Perhaps those agrobiologists were right who believed that the trend of the future would be toward smaller farms and more intensive yields. The relatively new science of farm chemurgy was revealing all sorts of new industrial uses for farm products; du Pont, for example, was using farm products in the making of cellophane, Duco, motion-picture film, rayon, pyralin, plastecele, fabrikoid, sponges, window shades, hair ornaments, handbags, alcohols, and a lot of other things which one would hardly associate with the old-fashioned farm. Yet even if the farmer of the future who applied new methods to the growing of specialized crops for specialized uses would be able to operate best with a small tract of land, as some people expected, would he be able to operate without more capital than most farmers possessed? That question was still unanswered.

Meanwhile large-scale tractor farming was spreading fast, and was repeating the harshness of mid-nineteenth-century industrialism—as if America had learned nothing in the interim.

How far would the new trend go? Would great mechanized farm corporations, perhaps controlled from the metropolitan cities, gradually put out of business the smaller farms of those rolling areas, such as abounded in the Old

Cotton South, where tractors could not readily be used?
Would the cotton picker invented by the Rust brothers of
Memphis accelerate this change? What would become, then,
of the already miserable sharecroppers? Were other parts of
the country destined sooner or later to go through the same
sort of transition that was taking place in the South and
West, producing a huge, roving landless proletariat of the
land, helpless if unorganized, menacing if organized because
it had no stake in the land and its settled institutions? These
questions, too, waited for answers.

Floods and Flood Control

For a generation or more the conservationists had been
warning the country that it was squandering its heritage of
land and forests and fields and minerals and animal life:
that in effect it was living riotously on its capital of national
resources. But to most citizens the subject had seemed dull,
academic. Now, in the Dust Bowl, the Lord had "taken a
hand" in instruction. And hardly had the black blizzards
blown themselves out when—as if distrustful whether the
country properly realized that droughts and floods were not
incompatible phenomena, but were associated results of
human misuse of the land—the Lord drove the lesson home.
The rivers went on a rampage.

"In 1936"—I quote from Stuart Chase's summary [in
Rich Land, Poor Land. Whittlesey House. 1936]—"the Mer-
rimac, Connecticut, Hudson, Delaware, Susquehanna, Potomac, Allegheny, and Ohio all went wild. The Potomac
was up twenty-six feet at Washington and long barriers of
sandbags protected government buildings. . . . Pittsburgh
was under ten to twenty feet of water and was without
lights, transport, or power. The life of 700,000 people was
paralyzed. The food supply was ruined, the steel industry at
a standstill." The following January, the unseasonably warm
and rainy January of 1937, the Ohio River produced what
was perhaps, all things considered, the worst flood in American history.

The bare facts of that flood are impressive. The Ohio rose 7.9 feet higher than it had ever risen before at Cincinnati, 6.8 feet higher than it had ever risen before at Louisville. Nine hundred people were estimated to have lost their lives by drowning or by other casualties resulting from the flood. The number of families driven from their homes was set at 500,000; the number still homeless a month after the worst of the crisis was set by the Red Cross at 299,000.

But these figures give no impression whatever of what men and women experienced in each town during the latter days of January as the swirling waters rose till the Ohio seemed a great rushing muddy lake full of floating wreckage, and the cold rain drizzled inexorably down, and every stream added its swollen contribution to the torrent. Railroad tracks and roads washed away. Towns darkened as the electric-light plants were submerged. Business halted, food supplies stopped, fires raging out of control, disease threatening. The city of Portsmouth, Ohio, opening six great sewer valves and letting seven feet of water rush into its business district, lest its famous concrete flood wall be destroyed. Cincinnati giving City Manager Dykstra dictatorial powers. The radio being used to direct rescue work and issue warnings and instructions to the population as other means of communication failed: a calm voice at the microphone telling rescuers to row to such-and-such an address and take a family off the roof, to row somewhere else and help an old woman out of a second-story window. Breadlines. The Red Cross, the Coast Guard, the WPA [Works Progress Administration] aiding in the work of rescue and reorganization. Martial law. Churches above the water line being used as refuges. Dead bodies of horses and cattle—yes, and of men and women—floating through the streets along with tree branches, gasoline tanks, beams from collapsed houses. Mud everywhere, as the waters receded—mud and stench. Most dramatic of all, perhaps, the triumphant fight to save Cairo, Illinois: men piling more and more sandbags atop the levee, standing guard day and night, rushing to strengthen the wall of defense wherever it weakened, as the waters rose and rose—and did not quite break over.

By this time everybody with any capacity for analysis was ready to begin to understand what the government technicians had long been saying in their monographs; what Stuart Chase and Paul B. Sears and David Cushman Coyle, the Mississippi Valley Committee and the National Resources Committee, and Pare Lorenz's very fine films, "The River" and "The Plough that Broke the Plains," were repeating in more popular terms: that floods as well as dust storms were largely the result of reckless misuse of the land. Indeed, as early as the beginning of 1936, when the Supreme Court threw out the Agricultural Adjustment Act, Congress took account of the new understanding in revamping its farm program. The new law was labeled a Soil Conservation and Domestic Allotment Act, and the new crop adjustments were called "soil-erosion adjustments."

Already at many points the government was at work restoring a deforested and degrassed and eroded countryside. In the CCC camps, young men were not only getting healthy employment, but were renewing and protecting the forest cover by planting trees, building firebreaks, removing inflammable underbrush, and building check dams in gullies. The experts of the Soil Conservation Service were showing farmers how to fight erosion by terracing, contour plowing, rotation of crops, strip cropping, and gully planting. After the dust storms, for example, they demonstrated how the shifting dunes of Dalhart, Texas, could be held in place by planting them with milo, Sudan grass, and black amber cane. Under the supervision of the Forest Service, the government between 1935 and 1939 planted 127 million trees to serve as windbreaks on the Great Plains. The Taylor Grazing Act of 1934 stopped homesteading on the great range and gave the Department of the Interior power to prevent overgrazing on eighty million acres.

PWA funds were going into the construction of dams which would aid in flood control (and also extend navigation), such as that at Fort Peck in eastern Montana, which was to create a lake 175 miles long. The TVA [Tennessee Valley Authority]—that most combative and most remarkable of the New Deal agencies—was not simply creating a new electric-light and power system in competition with privately owned utilities (though this part of its work stirred up ten times as much excitement as all the rest put together); its dams were also controlling floods, and it was showing farmers how to deal with erosion, how to use phosphates. (In 1937, during the Ohio River flood, the Tennessee River did not misbehave.) Other PWA funds were providing a better irrigation system for parts of Utah where water was running short. The colossal dam at Grand Coulee, Washington—the biggest thing ever built by man—was getting ready to pump water for the irrigation of 1.2 million acres of desert land, as well as to provide hydroelectric power in quantity (like its sister dam at Bonneville) for the future development of the Northwest. These were only a few of the numerous enterprises going ahead simultaneously.

Nor was the government undertaking these enterprises in a wholly piecemeal manner: through its National Resources Committee and other agencies it was making comprehensive studies of the country's resources and equipment, so that the movement of restoration and regeneration could proceed with a maximum of wisdom.

America Reaches Maturity

With the aid of these studies—and of the lessons taught by drought and flood—more and more Americans, during the latter 1930s, were beginning to see the problem of their country's future in a new light. They were beginning to realize that it had reached maturity. No longer was it growing hand-over-fist.

Immigration was no longer adding appreciably to its numbers: indeed, during the years between 1931 and 1936, the number of aliens *emigrating* from the United States had been larger each year than the number *immigrating*: the tide had actually been trickling in reverse. If, beginning in 1936, the incoming tide had increased again as Europeans sought to escape from the shadow of Hitlerism, even so the total remained tiny in comparison with those of prewar years. Ellis Island was no longer a place of furious activity. The time was at hand when the number of foreign-born people in the United States would be sharply diminished by death, and the sound of foreign languages would be heard less and less in the streets of American cities. Already the schools, the manufacturers of children's clothing, and the toy manufacturers were beginning to notice the effects of the diminished birth rate (accentuated by the sharp drop during the early Depression years). Writing in the spring of 1938, [social scientist] Henry Pratt Fairchild reported that there were over 1.6 million fewer children under ten in the United States than there had been five years earlier. School principals, confronting smaller entering classes of children, could well understand what the population experts were talking about when they predicted a slower and slower population growth for the country, with an increasing proportion of old people and a decreasing proportion of young ones. They could see the change taking place before their own eyes.

That the frontier was closed was not yet quite true, a generation of historians to the contrary notwithstanding; for the Northwest was still a land of essentially frontier possibilities. Yet for a long time past, young men and women bent on fortune had mostly been going, not west, but to the cities. If the victims of the Dust Bowl and the tractor had pushed west, their fate had been ironic. The brief return to the country of great numbers of jobless city dwellers during the early Depression years had only temporarily slowed down the movement from farm to city and town. For a long time past, the fastest-growing communities had been, by and large, not Western boom towns but the suburbs which ringed the big cities—and during the 1930s these suburbs were still adding to their numbers. Industry, by and large, was no longer moving westward; the great bulk of the country's manufacturing was still done along the north Atlantic seaboard and in the strip of territory running thence out through Pennsylvania and Ohio to Chicago and St. Louis—and some observers even believed they detected during the 1930s a slight shift back toward the East.

American individuals and families were becoming more nomadic. This was partly due to the omnipresence of the automobile; there were three million more cars on the road in 1937 than in 1929, for though fewer cars were sold, more old ones were still in use. Partly, as we have seen, it was due to the Depression search for jobs and to the eviction of farm tenants. But American *institutions* appeared, geographically, to be settling down.

Still there was a chance for a far richer development of the country, and the chance was most visible west of the Great Plains. Yet if this development was to be durable, the new pioneering must be more disciplined than the old. The hard fact that the days were over when Americans could plunder and move on, stripping off forests, ripping out minerals, and plowing up grasslands without regard to the long consequences, was now penetrating the public consciousness—even while the men and women whose farms had blown away were still wandering homeless through the land.

THE WAY OF THE FARMER [4]

With all the marvels of science in increasing energy sources and food abundance it is easy to forget that the final source of food is the land, and that the way of life on the land is the way of the farmer. This is not because of any deficiency of sentiment. Ever since Jefferson's dream of a society of free farmers, Americans have idealized the rural way of life, even while it was being displaced by the urban—

[4] From *America as a Civilization*, by Max Lerner, author, journalist, teacher of American history. Simon & Schuster. '57. 2v. v 1, p 139–47. Copyright © 1957 by Max Lerner. Reprinted by permission of Simon & Schuster, Inc.

perhaps exactly *because* it was being displaced. Many of the men in *Who's Who* come from farm backgrounds. It is not only the disproportionate political strength of the rural areas that gives farm-aid and crop-support programs an easy passage through Congress but also the folk-belief that the farmers form the nation's backbone and that there is somehow a healing grace and an elixir of sturdiness and integrity in contact with the soil which are not to be derived from contact with city pavements.

The way of the farmer, enthroned in American sentiment, has fared erratically in American reality. Until seventy-five years ago America was predominantly an agricultural economy, an agrarian polity, and a rural society. It is no longer any of the three. Fewer than twenty-two million, or only 13.5 percent of the population, lived on and from the land in 1955, as contrasted with 25 percent in 1930. Even while frontier lands were still accessible the proportion of farmers to the total working force kept dropping. Around 1825 three fourths of the gainfully employed Americans were on the farm; around 1875 the proportion was one half; in 1955 the farmers and farm workers comprised fewer than 7 million out of 65 million Americans with gainful jobs, or less than 11 percent. Of these 7 million, 3 million are farm workers, either hired men on small- and medium-sized farms, sharecroppers, or migratory workers on the large corporation farms of the West and Southwest. This leaves only some 4 million in the category of the independent farmer on the family-size farm. One should further subtract from this figure the "one-mule" cotton farmer and those still clinging to impoverished and eroded land and earning only the meagerest of submarginal livings from it. It was estimated in 1955 that between 800,000 and 1.75 million farm families were unable to earn a decent living on the land and would be better off if they were shifted to industry.

All this has been part of what Gilbert Burck, writing in *Fortune,* has called the "magnificent decline" of American agriculture. The quantitative decline is clear enough. In a quarter century, from 1930 to 1955, the number of farms shrank from 6.3 million to 5.2 million, with the likelihood that they would continue to shrink as the submarginal farms were pushed out. It was estimated that in another quarter century, by 1980, the 13.5 percent of the American people living on farms in 1955 would have become 8 percent, and extended far enough the curve would end in a small, professionalized group of firms running a highly mechanized and productive farm industry much as any other industry is run in America.

The "magnificent" element in the decline of American agriculture is to be found in the productivity gains. The break-through came late in the 1930s, largely because of the basic research on plant genetics, hybridization, and crossbreeding which has been done for years under the schools of agriculture and came to fruition under the New Deal; it was given impetus by World War II, and it reached its pitch in the decade from 1945 to 1955. In the latter year 37 percent less farm manpower produced 54 percent more than in 1930, and farm productivity had increased 110 percent in only a quarter century. The acreage remained relatively stable, and the man-hours decreased. What then made the difference? The answer lies in science and industrialization—in new forms of fertilizer, new hybrid breeds of corn, new ways of feeding hogs, new insecticides and pest controls, new methods of irrigation, new machinery, new capital investment, new techniques of business (cost accounting) management.

What has happened is that the sweep of the business spirit and of the machine has caught up the whole enterprise of farming and transformed it in the image of industrial enterprise. Far from being an overnight growth, mechanization has been a fact of American agriculture from the start. American farmers carried their initial crops and livestock over from Europe and made brilliant adaptations of them to the conditions of their own climate and soil. Scientific farming started in Europe and its techniques were used in England long before they were used in America. But the farm machinery, as embodied in the work of Whitney, McCormick, and Case, was America's own invention. The motorizing of the farm through the reaper, the threshing machine, the combine harvester, the multirow cultivator, and the cotton picker was largely the product of necessity, since there was plenty of land in a new country but a scarcity of labor. In Europe, where land was scarce and population crowded, the standard of progress was productivity per acre: it is still true that the intensive European agriculture gets an extremely high per-acre yield—but with a large expenditure of manpower. In America the standard of progress has been productivity per man-hour.

In recent years, however, the conquests of American farm machinery have been unparalleled. In 1935, American farms had a million tractors; in 1955 they had 4.5 million, along with 2.5 million trucks, almost a million combines, and three quarters of a million milking machines. The "motor revolution" was followed by an electrical revolution: in 1955 at least nine out of ten farms had electric power, as a result of the farsighted thinking of the founders of the Rural Electrification Administration—Morris L. Cooke and John Carmody, and the creative work of the electric cooperatives. Corn pickers in Iowa, haystackers in Montana, combines in the wheat country of Washington, potato harvesters on Long Island, citrus sprayers in Florida, cotton pickers in the South—these were the typical expressions of an investment of close to $20 billion in farm machinery. On a California corporate farm the "big-time growers" level the soil with bulldozers, spray it from airplanes, irrigate it with deep-well pumps, and get a yield of cotton per man-hour undreamed of in agricultural history. In the same spirit the hogs are fed by a nutrition calculus on a production-line basis, and the beef cattle are fattened with female sex hormones.

This has been called the coming of "automation" to the farm, which is inaccurate since human labor is still the indispensable factor in farming. Yet the march of mechanization on the farm is clear. A complex cotton-picking machine in 1955 did the work formerly done by sixty or seventy men. The small farmer, who cannot afford to operate on a scale to encompass it, is becoming an archaism. The average size of the American farm in 1955 was 215 acres, and if the submarginal farms were not counted it was much higher. About two million American farms, grossing $2,500 a year, formed the heart of the farm operations. The bigger farmer, able to invest in machinery, has shaken his spear across the land. Were Thomas Jefferson to come back, with his dream of a small-scale agrarian America, he would turn in dismay from what would seem to him a monster of technocracy—man-hour productivity, chemical and hormone science, production-line efficiency, high capital investment, and motor and electrical mechanization.

Thus the machine and its camp followers have gone far to transform the way of the farmer. His relation to science, industrialism, and business power has changed. The lines of energy now flow from the center, once represented by the small independent farmer, toward the big farmer and the corporate farm, with its massive, impersonal organization: yet one cannot ignore the less characteristic submarginal farmer, the sharecropper on tired soil, the migratory hired field worker.

The Independent Farmer Is Disappearing

The independent farmer as the "masterless man" has dwindled in importance. He may still be found growing corn in Kansas and steers and hogs in Iowa, potatoes in Maine or on Long Island, or grazing cattle in Wyoming. His wife is peerless at baking pies and putting up preserves, which she now does in an electrically equipped kitchen; his children belong to the 4-H clubs (Head, Heart, Hands, Health), raise blue-ribbon fair winners of their own, play basketball at high school, attend land-grant universities, drive cars and tractors, and study science; he is usually a

Republican (except in periods of steeply falling prices), a churchgoer, a moviegoer, a TV-set owner, a book-club subscriber, reader of *Life, Time, Newsweek, Look,* and the *Reader's Digest,* a member of the Farm Bureau or the Grange, a political power in his community. Yet he is not, as he was in Jefferson's or Jackson's time or even [William Jennings] Bryan's, the bulwark of the American community.

In looking at the splendid efficiency of the best American farming, it is easy to forget how much of it rides on the backs of humble, anonymous men. In California, for example, there were over a half million farm workers; through the whole Southwest (although their number was recently reduced) there were still swarms of Mexican-American "wetbacks," or illegals, who swam the Rio Grande at night, turning the border into a sieve, and had to be rounded up periodically and deported by airlift; and there were many contract workers, some of whom settled down as American citizens, while some came and returned each year. In California's San Joaquin and Imperial valleys the corporate farms, which were once described by Carey McWilliams as "factories in the field," have improved considerably in their condition; yet their workers are not included in federal security and social legislation, are still paid submarginal wages, and buy their food from company commissaries.

In the South also it would be hard to talk of the "independent farmer." The South suffered in the past from being a one-crop region, where Cotton was King until very recently, when agriculture became more diversified. With other countries now growing cotton, America's share of the world market decreased sharply, and the pressures were toward efficiency. In the Mississippi Delta, in Texas, in some areas of Alabama, cotton growing was mechanized on a large scale, feasible only for the "plantation farms" or for those with capital to invest or for cooperatives banding together to buy farm machinery. The small cotton grower of the South, a victim of high labor cost on the unmechanized one-mule farm, and of the boll weevil and debt, is on the way out. On the eroded soil only the wretched living standards of the submarginal croppers and subsistence farmers and on the good soil only the mechanized and large-scale farms are now possible.

I do not mean to give the impression of backwardness on the American soil. Compare the American farmer with the Malayan or Indonesian peasant—impoverished, sick, undernourished, badly housed and clothed, a prey to the usurer, without incentive, tilling land he does not own—and the contrast is dramatic. Take the family-size farm in the mixed-farming areas of Ohio, Wisconsin, Minnesota, Illinois, and in the corn-wheat-hog and prime-beef areas of Kansas, Iowa, Nebraska, and the Dakotas, and compare it with the European peasantry that exasperated Karl Marx into talking of "rural idiocy" and of the farmer as a primitive "troglodyte": again the contrast is dramatic.

Yet every system of agriculture pays its own kind of social price for the methods it uses. In the late nineteenth century much of American farming was a kind of soil mining which stripped the land while it made production cheap. (Incidentally, by undercutting the more highly priced British agriculture of the time and selling their food cheaply in England, the Americans almost killed British farming.) At present the highly organized and rationalized nature of American farming carries with it a different kind of social price. The acreage under cultivation has remained steady while the number of farms and farmers has decreased. The traditional "hired man," who was close to the farmer's family, is disappearing and is being displaced by migrants and machine tenders in the fields and in the dairy. Landlessness has become a reality: there are the landless croppers and tenants, the landless Negroes, the landless seasonal workers. The reach of landlessness grows in direct proportion to the reach of mechanization. California, for example, where agriculture developed late and as part of the machine era, shows the clearest cleavage between the controllers of the mechanized corporate farms and the landless casual laborers whose situation is worse than that of the machine tenders in the factories because they have no unions, are not protected by social legislation, and lack access to the leisure activities and the popular culture of urban life.

One may grow unduly sentimental about the disappearance of the Jeffersonian image of the farmer on his soil, and of the old family-size farm that was not part of the machine technology. "The truth is," wrote Louis Bromfield, "that farming as a way of life is infinitely more pleasurable and satisfactory when it is planned, scientific, specialized, mechanized, and stripped of the long hours and the drudgery of the old-fashioned, obsolete pattern of the frontier or general farm." This has always been the case for agricultural rationalization. Yet it cannot obscure the fact that the old love of the soil has been replaced by a fetishism of output, efficiency, and cost accounting. This is already evident in the arguments of the efficiency-minded agricultural experts who say that the small, "inadequate" farmer will simply have to get off the land. What applies now to the small farmer is bound in time to apply to the middle-sized farmer. The logic of this latter-day advance of capitalism upon the land is as unyielding as in the case of the historical enclosure movements. The fact that the victims of the large-scale expulsion from the land are being absorbed in industry does not make it any less expulsion.

Farming and the Capitalist Economy

There is a striking paradox at the heart of the relation between farming and the American capitalist economy. On the one hand farming has become thoroughly mechanized and industrialized and has thus become part of the larger wide-flung economy: the farmer, purchasing chemicals and machinery on a large scale and applying them to the land, has become largely a processor. On the other hand, farming is the only large sector of the economy—apart from national defense—that is subsidized and thus stands apart from the rest of the economy.

There are two basic reasons for this dependent state. One is the limited expansionism of the demand for farm products. Even with the "eating revolution" and the new habits of the American worker in consuming meats and dairy products, the rise in living standards does not mean a proportionate rise in food consumption. What is true of the home market for industry—that lower production cost has led to larger demand, the rise of new industries, and the indefinite expansion of old ones—is thus not true of farming. The second factor is that farm prices are fluctuating prices, and historically the fluctuations have been violent and the farmer has been at their mercy. In high-price periods, especially war periods, the American farmer historically gave way to his land hunger, and in an expansionist spree he mortgaged himself to buy up more land and nourish his pride of ownership. In low-price periods he was wiped out.

That is one reason why the "farm problem" was finally stabilized by making the farmer in a sense the ward of the state—by price support, parity payments, crop restriction, acreage control, "soil bank," and government purchase and storing of the farmer's surplus so that he would not again be the victim of the price fluctuations of the free-enterprise system. Another reason was the failure of farm income to keep pace either with the advance of the national income as a whole or with industrial prices. In 1929 the farmer's share of the national income was 7 percent; in 1954 it had fallen to 4 percent. Roughly it doubled in that period, but the national income increased fourfold. The position of the marginal farmer made the situation worse. By the 1950 census figures, over a million and a half farm families had a cash income of less than $1,000 a year, mostly on eroded or poor soil, or on sandy soil on the coastal plain, or on tiny tracts in the South. Even the national average farm income was less than $4,000 per farm—which was low when compared with nonfarm income in America, although very high when compared with farmers in other countries.

The farmer used his massive political strength—far disproportionate to his numbers—to get government price supports which would balance these inequities and give his income some stability. Although the original policies of price support developed out of the New Deal, no Republican Administration has dared abandon them. In 1955 there was a $7 billion surplus of farm products under government price support. The granaries and storage space were full to bursting. The efforts to ease the problem by finding foreign markets were necessarily limited by the adverse effect of dumping policies on American foreign relations. The efforts at acreage reduction were also futile, since they were easily evaded, and the productivity was rising higher than the acreage decrease.

The "Rural Mind"

There has been a good deal of discussion of the American "rural mind," but it is hard to talk of it as if it were a single entity. The "mind" of the Arena Imperial Company is different from that of an Iowa corn farmer, which in turn is different from that of a Maine potato farmer, or an Alabama "red-neck" or Georgia "cracker" or "wool hat," and all in turn are different from the mind of an Arkansas Negro cropper, a Rio Grande Valley wetback, or a Jamaican or Puerto Rican contract laborer on the Eastern truck garden or tobacco farms. The mind of a corn-belt farmer is different from that of a cotton-belt farmer, a wheat-belt farmer, a Wisconsin or Pennsylvania or New York dairy farmer, a Rocky Mountain range cattle grazer or sheep grazer, a Florida or California citrus grower. Economic, sectional, ethnic, and class variations, not to speak of individual differences, cut across the conditionings of the farm life itself.

Are there common elements forming what may still be called the farmer's outlook? Veblen thought it was precapitalist and "animistic," due to the farmer's having been bypassed by the technology—and therefore by the psychology —of the machine; that the farmer was conservative because he dealt with a physical environment he could neither calculate nor control, and that he was therefore more inclined to a belief in the magical aspects of social institutions than the industrial worker whose animism had been rubbed away by habituation to the machine.

The trouble with this view—aside from its ignoring of the later machine revolution on the farm—is that it turns the facts of American history on their head. It was the farmers who were associated with the historical American movements of political protest and dissent. From Shays' Rebellion to the twenty-four-hour violence of the farm-holiday movement of the Great Depression, earlier American radicalism was largely agrarian. This radicalism may have been an assertive opposition to the business power the farmers saw challenging them, and their Populism from Bryan's time to [Robert] La Follette's may have been a last stand against the monopolists who had taken over both the economy and the government. Agrarian radicalism always had in it a strong sense of property and traditionalism: the Populists wanted more to recapture an imaginary agricultural independence than to create new conditions. It was also a radicalism which found room for a heavy component of isolationism and anti-Semitism, as the currents of thought showed in the late 1930s. But it would be hard in any event to maintain Veblen's thesis of the farmer's conservatism in American history.

What was the source of this radicalism and why did it all but disappear? The core of the farmer's attitude has been a fierce individualism. As individualism became more and more linked with the anti-interventionist antibureaucratic doctrines of Republican conservatism, the farmers became the great conservative force of America. The Granger Revolt, the Farmers' Alliance, the Farmer-Labor parties, the Non-Partisan leagues, the Populist and Progressive groups whose center was in the agricultural states of the Middle West, were largely ironed out of the American political picture. The "sons of the wild jackass" who used to come to Congress from the Midwestern states are no more. This does not mean the Republicans can always count on the "farm vote." The elections for a twenty-year period, from 1932 through 1952, showed that the farmer shops around for price supports. But his basic conservatism of outlook survived the New Deal and Fair Deal. Strikingly, this change from agrarian radicalism to agrarian conservatism became more pronounced with the mechanization of agriculture. In the case of the farmers, [Thorsten] Veblen's "discipline of the machine" has worked in an inverse way. It would be more to the point to say that the farmer grew more conservative as his living standard rose.

The farmer's individualism had its roots in the fact that, except for the corporate farms and the co-ops, the farmer has to wrestle with soil and climate, bugs and boll weevils, chemistry and hormones, largely by himself. It is not that he deals (in Veblen's terms) with "magic" but that whatever he deals with he has to deal with as an individual enterpriser: the directness of effort and reward, the Lockean sense of property as whatever a man has acquired by mixing his sweat with the soil, are as nakedly manifested in the family farm as in small-scale business enterprise. This has made both of them areas of individualism.

American Farmer Not a Village-Dweller

In one respect the American farmer differs from farmers all over the world. He is not a village-dweller. In India, for example, three quarters of the population lives in the traditional farm village. The European village-community might conceivably have been transferred to America and for a time in New England—while the dangers from the Indians were still felt—the farmers huddled together. But except for the Mormon settlements in Utah and the village culture of the Spanish-speaking groups in the Southwest, the way of the American farmer is to live on his farm homestead and leave the village and town to the traders, farm-implement dealers, grain and feed dealers, storekeepers, mill-workers, and service groups. The decisive historical moment here came in the settlement of the Middle West. The Homestead Acts required residence on the land to support the title: the typical homestead was a "quarter section" of 160 acres, which meant that the farmers lived scattered over the land, separated by far distances, with a one-room schoolhouse for their children and a small church set in the open country for their worship. The difficulties of transport kept the farm community within the distance of the "team haul." The result was a fierce localism which laid its stress on local autonomy, a fear of statism, an isolated way of life that led to isolationism in outlook. The farmer's relation to the town was one of hostility: it was the relation of a producer to the middleman who bought his products cheap, and the storekeepers who sold him other products dear; it was the relation of the debtor to the banker, the creditor, the mortgage-holder. This increased his individualism, his isolationism, his burning sense of grievance.

Life has changed for the independent farmer, whether in the Midwest or elsewhere. He has come into a new relation to the standardizing forces of American culture and has become part of the communications revolution. The automobile, the radio, movies, and TV have brought him out of his isolation; he does his shopping and trading less in the farm village and more in the larger industrial center where he can get spare parts for his machinery and the newest fashions for his wife and daughters. His one-room schoolhouse has become a consolidated school located in the trade center to which his children ride daily on a school bus; his land is no longer heavily mortgaged; his crops are price-supported by the federal government, and in raising them he gets the help of government technicians. The work of a farmer is still hard, heavy work, and the risks of weather and market fluctuations are still real risks. But as farming has become a subsidized sector of the economy, and the security of the farmer one of the tasks of the welfare state, his antistatism is shown up as an anachronism. Nevertheless as a traditional "agin-er," it is still as logical for him to be "agin" the state which subsidized him as it was for him to be "agin" the system of business power which organized the home-market and world-market demand for his products.

In most areas of the world the rural population is custom-bound. In the United States custom has largely loosened its hold, and the farmer is battered by all the dislocating forces of contemporary life. What used to be called the "rural community" has been churned up and is to be found across the country in various stages of disorganization. There has been a steady movement away from the land. The farmer's daughter who has been to the university moves to the towns and cities for marriage or a career; the farmer's son who has gone to an agricultural college sometimes stays to manage the farm, sometimes is drawn away by the more powerful suction force of city life. The slack is taken up by bigger farm units and by corporate management.

The pull of the farm has not vanished: every year there are young Americans who would like to take up farming as a way of life, but the only available government land is the small tracts of Western public lands newly reclaimed by irrigation, and the waiting list for each is a long one. A more important trend is that of the man with a career in the city who likes to farm as a supplementary way of life (much like the English gentleman of the eighteenth and nineteenth centuries) and can afford the investment it requires—and in many cases writes the loss off against his high-bracket income tax. He is another example of how the farmer's way has been swept up into the powerful sway of the pecuniary culture of America.

THE DECLINE OF THE SMALL TOWN [5]

The American place started with small population units, rapidly grew to big ones, and has ever since been under

[5] From *America as a Civilization*, by Max Lerner, author, journalist, teacher of American history. Simon & Schuster. '57. 2v. v 1 p 148–55. Copyright © 1957 by Max Lerner. Reprinted by permission of Simon & Schuster, Inc.

the double tension of moving from the small unit to the big one and at the same time moving from the center of the bigger unit outward toward the rim. Traditionally the small town has been held to embody the American spirit better than the larger frame. De Tocqueville affirmed that the township as a unit both of government and of living had preceded the state and nation in America and was more important than either. In New England the township has lasted over three hundred years, and while it has been battered by heavy pressures from state, nation, and economy, it still retains traces of the two goods that Americans have always seen in it—the friendliness of face-to-face relations and the concern about the town's affairs felt by all its citizens.

De Tocqueville had a reason of his own for his tub-thumping about the New England township—his hatred for French centralization, which made a person

a kind of settler, indifferent to the fate of the spot which he inhabits. The greatest changes are effected there without his concurrence. . . . The condition of his village, the police of his street, the repairs of the church or parsonage, do not concern him; for he looks upon all these things as unconnected with himself and as the property of a powerful stranger whom he calls the government.

He saw American town government as the ideal contrast to this lugubrious picture. For all his bias he was nonetheless right about the "provincial independence" of the American small town and the fierce identification of even its poorest citizens with the disputes and rivalries that raged about its affairs. This intensity still prevails in many New England towns, governed by three Selectmen, who draw up annual budgets that are examined, item for item, by the entire citizenry sitting in the primary democracy of the town meeting. In the early days of the Republic the small town was the tap spring of the revolutionary spirit and of cultural strength. There were few Presidents from Lincoln and

Grant to Truman and Eisenhower who were not the products of small-town culture. During most of American history, until the turn of the twentieth century, it was the basic community form for most Americans.

But the growing point of American life is scarcely to be found in the small town today. Latterly the important lines of growth have been elsewhere. It is partly that all the small units in American life are having to wage a losing fight—not only the small town but the small farm, the small business firm, the small college, even the neighborhood within the big city. Somewhere between the turn of the century and the New Deal the small town felt the withering touch of the Great Artifact that we call American society, and in the quarter century between 1930 and 1955 the decisive turn was made, away from small-town life. The currents of American energy moved around and beyond the small towns, leaving them isolated, demoralized, with their young people leaving them behind like abandoned ghost towns.

What happened was that the small town lost its economic and cultural base. Partly this happened in the areas most badly scarred by soil erosion, where the destruction of the rural hinterland stripped away the substance of small-town existence. But actually this was a marginal force. Everywhere, even in the most prosperous areas, the small town was undercut by the big changes in American life—the auto and superhighway, the supermarket and the market center, the mail-order house, the radio and TV, the growth of national advertising, the mechanization of farming—so that it turned its face directly to the centers of technology. It was the city and the suburb—the cluster-city complex—that became the focus of working and living, consuming and leisure. "None of the kids ever come back here to live after they've gone away to school," said an older man from Shannon Center, Iowa, which had lost almost half its population in the 1940s. The young people go on to find jobs in factories or businesses far from where they grew up, or they go away to college or technical school and get the kind of training for which the small town, with its limited opportunities, simply cannot offer a demand.

What Is a Small Town?

I have been talking here of an entity hard to define, especially in drawing a line between the small town and the city. The Census Bureau calls any community of over 2,500 people "urban," and for 1950 showed some 3,000 communities in America with a population between 1,000 and 2,500; more than 3,000 with a population from 2,500 to 10,000; and 3,800 with a population between 2,500 and 25,000. One might put the dividing line at around 10,000 or 15,000 people, but it would be an arbitrary line.

The test is at what point the town grows too big to make life compassable. The value of small-town living lies in the face-to-face relations that it makes possible throughout the community. One might say that a small town ceases to be one as soon as someone who has lived in it a number of years finds unfamiliar faces as he walks down the street and is not moved to discover who they are and how they got there. For in a small town it is the unfamiliar that is remarkable, just as in a big city the memorable experience is to meet in a random walk through the streets someone you know. It has occurred to more than one observer that if a big-city inhabitant were to respond to all the people he meets to the same degree as a small-town inhabitant, he would end as a raving lunatic.

One notes that most of the communities in the spate of recent surveys (the Newburyport of Lloyd Warner's *Yankee City,* the Morris of his *Democracy in Jonesville,* the Natchez of John Dollard's *Caste and Class in a Southern Town,* the Grafton of Granville Hicks's *Small Town*) were about towns of less than 25,000. Muncie of the *Middletown* studies by Robert and Helen Lynd (38,000 at the time of the first study, 48,000 at the second) was somewhat larger. Each study was an effort to catch the distillation of American life through a microscopic analysis of a cross section of it. Clearly, the small town lends itself most easily to this kind of inductive study because it is small enough to grasp. But I doubt the symbolic value it is intended to have for America as a whole. What the studies are discovering is the America of an earlier generation. The changes operative in the growth centers of American life are reflected in distorted form in the small town, like the shadows in Plato's cave.

The idea that the small town is the seed ground of what is characteristically American has not been restricted to its glorifiers or to the survey-makers. It may be found in so hostile a critic as Thorstein Veblen, in his classic essay on The Country Town (*Absentee Ownership in America*). He wrote as an agrarian radical of the Scandinavian Midwest, resenting the Yankee merchants and bankers who had come from New England to take over the Great Plains. He saw in the country town the roots of the capitalist attitude—the "predatory" and "prehensile" spirit of American business enterprise, middleman rather than producer, quick to discern a profit, greedy to grasp it, tenacious in holding on to it. It was ruthless evaluation yet not without its insight. A history of American industry will show how many of the men who came to the top of the heap spent their formative years in the small town and in many instances got their business start there. But even when Veblen wrote in the mid-1920s the small town was ceasing to be the focus of the capitalist spirit.

The fact that the small town is dwindling in importance makes Americans idealize it all the more. The phrase *small town* has come itself to carry a double layer of meaning, at once sentimental and condescending. There is still a belief that democracy is more idyllic at the "grass roots," that the business spirit is purer, that the middle class is more intensely middling. There is also a feeling that by the fact of being small the small town somehow escapes the corruptions of life in the city and the dominant contagions that infest the more glittering places. History, geography, and economics gave each American town some distinctive traits of style that are imbedded in the mind, and the memory of this style is all the more marked because of the nostalgia felt, in a largely urban America, for what seems the lost serenity of small-town childhoods.

This was probably part of the basis for the "Renaissance" of the small town at mid-century, just when its decay and the movement of population from it were most marked. There was a return to it emotionally, if not intellectually, as a repository of the older and more traditional values. A number of writers, advertising men, newspapermen, and artists dreamed of forsaking the competitive tensions of New York, Chicago, or Hollywood to settle down in a small town and find the abandoned "heart of America." In the university centers some of the professors made heroic efforts to revive the energies of the small town and recapture its control for the people, much as the Russian *Narodniki* [Populists] at the turn of the century dreamed of "going to the people" and finding among them new strength with which to grapple with the tasks of social revolution and reconstruction.

The question few of them faced was why the small town had declined and been rejected by the younger people. One might have expected the face-to-face quality of its living and the strong personal ties it afforded to have served as an attraction to young families settling down to a tranquil and satisfying way of life. But this reckons without the counterforce of recoil from the torpor and tyranny of the small town. The best clue to this counterforce showed up in the literature of the 1910s and 1920s—in the portrait of Spoon River in Edgar Lee Masters' poems, in the Gopher Prairie of Sinclair Lewis's *Main Street,* in the bitter narratives of Sherwood Anderson and Theodore Dreiser. As early as 1882 Ed Howe had laid bare the meanness and sterility of small-town life in *The Story of a Country Town.* All these writers depicted mercilessly the provincialism of small-town life, the stifling constraints, the sense of stagnation that came from living in a closed room. It is unlikely that the forces of American conformism were more cruelly displayed anywhere than in the heavy hand that the small town habitually laid on the man or woman who too rashly broke the moral code. Just as heavy was the hand one laid on one's own rebel impulses. The record at once of the outer social tyranny and the inner repression may be read in the stony faces of Grant Wood's provincials.

Even the efforts at "reform" were part of the mood of disillusionment. Carol Kennicott, who tried to bring culture to Gopher Prairie, was in the line of succession of the women who had founded the Minerva Clubs, the Ladies' History Clubs, and the Ladies' Library Associations of Sioux Falls, South Dakota, and Weeping Waters, Nebraska, and Sleepy Eye, Minnesota, seeking to bring culture to the moving frontier. Yet while Carol was not new, she expressed a change of mood. Sinclair Lewis, like Masters, Dreiser, and Anderson, drew for much of his creativeness upon his smoldering rebellion against the "lassitude and futility" of Gopher Prairie. Its Main Street, he wrote, "is the continuation of Main Streets everywhere." And he added, with his heavy satiric underscoring, "Main Street is the climax of civilization"—although it is worth adding that in his later novels Lewis reversed his position and took back his satire. His fellow townsmen were meanwhile content with Main Street. "Somehow Harry Lewis didn't like it here," was the way one of his boyhood friends from Sauk Center put it many years later. But this was no crotchet of Lewis's: it was true of other writers and artists. The city revolution had brought with it a widening of horizons and a dislocation of social ties. The sensitive ones who were left behind felt cheated of life.

A number of critics, including T. S. Eliot, have linked creative achievement with the face-to-face relations possible in a small community. This may be so, but in the United States the poets and novelists of the period wrote as they did, not because they had ties with the small town but because they were breaking their ties. The creatively releasing force for them was the sense of breaking through the encrusted mold of custom. The very smallness of the small town gave them compassable symbols of grievance and hatred, and it dramatized both the clash between the small town and the Great Society and also the sense of breakthrough. Even in the 1950s many young men writing their first novels chose the macrocosm of some small town to depict. . . . But in a sense the 1920s saw "the last of the provincials," as Maxwell Geismar put it, and the great writing moved away from the small town and its life to the city and its suburbs and the outside world.

What Happened to the Small Town?

What happened to the small town was not only that the big social changes undercut it and swirled around it, leaving it isolated, but they also drained it of its store of power. The power of America today is to be found largely with the business and community leaders of the city, who initiate policies for corporate empires, trade-unions, national pressure groups, and big-audience media. Knowing this, we tend to forget that in an earlier America the decisions that expressed the American will were largely made by small-town lawyers, bankers, merchants, editors. As merchandizing, transport, and recreation shifted, the locus of power shifted. The town could no longer perform most of its functions alone—roadbuilding, relief, education, taxation, public works—and it came to depend on subsidies from the federal and state governments. As the power diminished, however, the intensity of the feuds and rivalries did not always subside, and the small town sometimes offered the unreal spectacle of an intensified struggle over dwindling stakes of power.

To the outward eye, the town of the 1950s, with its church spires, its Town Hall, its Main Street stores, its bank, its weekly newspaper, seemed what it always was. But its decay was unmistakable, taking the form of a displacement of its power and a disorganization of its traditional ways of life. Charles Francis Adams had seen it generations earlier, in his poetic description (in *Three Episodes of Massachusetts History*) of the disappearance of the New England village. Even the close controls which the code-makers of the town once exerted on its moral standards had to be relaxed in the face of the general moral confusion. [Sociologist] George Homans pointed out, in commenting on a study of the social disorganization of "Hilltown"—a Massachusetts farming town of about 1,000 people —that a town clerk who absconded with community funds was no longer dealt with draconically as in similar cases in the past, that girls being dated were expected to "come across" sexually, and that virginity before marriage was no longer stressed or counted upon. Few would argue today that the condition of mental health in the small town is better than in the city, or that there is less alcoholism or a better family situation. Nor can one any longer underplay the seamier sides of American localism—the heartbreaking inertia, the presence of corruption and greed even at the grass roots. Human meanness and human generosity are widely distributed in a culture, and the pursuit of the cultural life goals goes on with little reference to the unit of living. There may be greater tranquillity in the small town but no more happiness; there are face-to-face relations but no deeper understanding of the human situation; there is a more compassable universe to grasp, physically and socially, but in reality it is no less bewildering.

The Problem of Place in America

If I have been unsparing here in dealing with the legend of small-town superiority, I do not mean to belittle the enduring although lesser place the small town is likely to have in American life. The growth of a highly urban and mechanized Great Society has by-passed not only the town itself but also some of the values with which it was historically linked. Emerson's Concord, Lincoln's Springfield, William Allen White's Emporia, Truman's Independence, and Eisenhower's Abilene must have borne along on their current a way of life strong enough to shape the men they produced. Some of America's towns, especially in New England and in the prosperous areas of the Middle West, are still conscious of being the carriers of a tradition and a philosophy. When Harry Truman, commenting on the problem of juvenile delinquency, wrote that "our children need fewer gadgets and more chores," he was expressing a recognizable small-town philosophy—the direct, no-nonsense, keep-life-simple philosophy of small-town mores. Truman's own personality—informal, downright, salty, with its strong sense of task, its stress on personal loyalties and obligations, its rejection of cant, its shrewd assessment of men and issues, and its built-in moral code—is the distillation of what is healthiest and most pungent in the surviving values of small-town culture. Although most small-town politicians (and much of American politics still derives from the small town) would shy away from Truman's identification with majority aspirations and minority causes, with labor interests and civil liberties and Negro civil rights, enough of them are enough like Truman to make a fusion of urban and small-town values conceivable. If the small town is wholly sacrificed there will be sacrificed along with it some continuity of face-to-face relations, an awareness of identity, a striving to be part of a compassable whole, a sense of counting for something and being recognized as a person and not a cipher.

A number of recent American writings indicate that the nostalgia for the small town need not be construed as directed toward the town itself: it is rather a "quest for community" (as Robert Nisbet puts it)—a nostalgia for a compassable and integral living unit. The critical question is not whether the small town can be rehabilitated in the image of its earlier strength and growth—for clearly it cannot—but whether American life will be able to evolve any other integral community to replace it. This is what I call the problem of place in America, and unless it is somehow resolved, American life will become more jangled and fragmented than it is, and American personality will continue to be unquiet and unfulfilled.

If the small town survives at all in a future America, it will have to survive within this frame and on a new economic base—not as the minor metropolis of a farming area, or as a mill town or mining town, but as a fusion of farming and industrial life along with the residential spill-over from the city and the suburb. It is worth saying here that neither the mammoth city nor the dormitory suburb is as it stands an adequate solution of the problem of place in America. Neither is the small town as it stands. But it can diversify its economic base, especially with the trend toward decentralizing industry. With the new modes of transport it can reach even the distant big city easily—for work or recreation, school, medical facilities, or friends. And it can build a way of life which forms a continuity with the small town of the past but without its cluttering accompaniments of provincialism and torpor.

POLITICAL INFLUENCE OF THE FARM BLOC [6]

A more respected and equally useful function is performed by the pressure groups and by their agents. A pressure group may represent a permanent economic or social interest, or the sponsors or opponents of a particular piece of legislation or administrative policy. They may want to protect migratory birds, or the Indians, or national monuments like Mount Vernon, to ban lascivious films or get federal aid for schools. Every important church, every important "movement" is a pressure group and it has its agents and offices in Washington. . . .

[6] From *Politics in America*, by D. W. Brogan, British writer and teacher, expert on American history and politics. Harper. '54; (Anchor Books) Doubleday. paper ed. '60. p 304–10. Copyright 1954 by D. W. Brogan. Reprinted by permission of Harper & Row, Publishers, Inc.

The first of these is what used to be called in England the agricultural interest. The most sacred if not the most important of the pressure groups is that vaguely called the farmers. They are important for several reasons. They are numerous, far more numerous than in Britain. They represent a very important segment of the economy. They are politically stronger than their numbers justify in the House of Representatives and still stronger in the Senate. And, perhaps as weighty as the other reasons for the attention paid to their demands, the farmers are *sacred*.

It was the belief of the founders of the Republic that the farmers were the salt of the earth. If Jefferson's dream of a republic of virtuous husbandmen was beginning to be merely a dream by the time of his death, it remained a potent myth. From the farmers came the men who made America. "From log cabin to White House" was a well-traveled road. It was profitable for a politician to have a rural background and to continue to have one. More politicians than one described themselves, as a cynic noted, as "farmers," because "they had one cow and twenty banks." But despite the praise and indeed adulation lavished on the farmer, he did not do so well materially as he did spiritually. He was told of his happy lot, but repeatedly refused to accept it. . . .

Farm discontent became a feature of the American political landscape. Organizations of all kinds sprang up to represent him and to lobby for him. The oldest still active is the Grange, the "Patrons of Husbandry." This body originally aimed at elevating the farmer intellectually and morally as well as financially. It tried to give the farmer a rural ethos as well as tangible material reward for his public-spirited activities.

The Grange, however, is no longer an effective national lobby. Its lodge buildings are more likely to be found in the diversified farming regions of New England raising dairy cattle, market garden crops, and tourists, than in the basic-crop regions of the Middle West. More important is the

Farm Bureau Federation which, basically, represents the grain and cotton areas. It represents, too, the more prosperous and conservative farmers and, in fact though no longer in form, it is in close contact with the state agricultural extension services, an alliance that gives the Farm Bureau the inside track in farm politics in many states. The National Farmers' Union is a more radical though not very radical alliance of the less prosperous farmers, the heir of the old agrarian radicals of the nineteenth century.

All of these groups dabble in politics, but there is not, at the moment in America, an open, united agrarian movement of the type that in the past repeatedly led the embattled farmers into usually fruitless battles for their rights. The early "Grangers," the Alliance, the farm cooperatives, the Non-Partisan League, represented a different approach to farm politics than that favored by the farm lobbies of today. The most radical and the most interesting of the organizations that sought to capitalize the discontent of the farmers was the Non-Partisan League. Its center was in the wheat belt, above all in North Dakota, whose farmers were most exposed to the vicissitudes of the market, had a remarkably homogeneous, mainly Scandinavian-American culture and were the victims of the last great expansion of the arable frontier, just as the expanding market for grain began to sag and then collapse. The title of the League revealed its aim, to circumvent the established party system, and it was helped in this by the impact of the first war on communities that were either neutral in spirit, like the Scandinavians, or for American neutrality if not neutral themselves, as were the Germans. And there were few or no industries to weaken the conviction that the farmer was the salt of the earth, his way of life almost the only human way of life.

League leaders pointed to agriculture as "the most important industry under the shining sun." Emperors, kings, ministers, presidents, parliaments, congresses, great generals, mighty armies with monster guns and forests of bayonets and mountains of shot and shell are down on their knees before the man with the hoe. Yet, he has had but little direct voice in affairs of government that determine his weal or woe. Men who can hardly tell the difference between a cotton boll and a chrysanthemum, are expected to legislate for the most vital industry of all. . . . The case of the North Dakota farmers was but one instance where "the farmers had been vainly begging a bunch of wind-jamming, booze-fighting politicians for legislation to protect them against the flour-mill trust and the grain gamblers." [*Agricultural Discontent in the Middle West*, by Theodore Saloutos and J. D. Hicks]

But although the League had its moments of success, its experiments in state socialism broke down and it simply added a variation to the political organization of the Middle West and provided a political springboard for politicians like former Senator Gerald Nye [Republican, North Dakota] and [former] Senator William Langer [Republican, North Dakota].

More promising was the farm bloc composed of middle western and southern members of Congress, candidly out for what they could get for their interests and their sections. After the first war, the farm bloc had some success if only in upsetting the conservative high command of the Republican party. But all attempts to get Congress to do something substantial for the farmer failed. He could not, in presidential elections, be wooed away from the GOP [the Republican party], and the Republican leaders saw no real reason for doing anything substantial for him, apart from giving him useless tariff protection. With the New Deal, came a different attitude and, before many years were out, it was discovered that what the farmer wanted was high prices for his crops paid in cash; whether they were paid by the consumer as consumer or as taxpayer, became more and more a matter of indifference to the farmers. After being at the "little end of the horn" for generations, the farmer became, if not the pampered pet of the federal government, at any rate the chief visible beneficiary of federal bounty. His crops were supported by the government which bought them when they fell below a fixed price level. This

kept the prices up and, in some cases, priced his farm products out of the market. Great quantities of foodstuffs were
stored in federal granaries and on the farms; the little metal
storehouses, like miniature gasometers, dotted the landscape; and it was the belief that the Republican eightieth
Congress was opposed to providing adequate storing facilities and so to getting just prices for the farmer, that turned
some middle western states in favor of Mr. Truman in 1948.

Since that political earthquake, politicians have been
more than nervous in dealing with the farmers and the degree to which politicians have been intimidated makes the
enactment of a rational farm policy almost impossible. Yet
the farmers are no more a block of identical interests than
are businessmen and possibly less than is labor. The various spokesmen for the farmers represent very different economic levels and interests and what suits the Farm Bureau
Federation need not and usually does not suit the Farmers'
Union and not always even the Grange.

The Union, as the avowed champion of the poor family
farmer, has pitted itself against the Farm Bureau Federation as
the alleged champion of the large-scale commercial producer.
According to the Union and its sympathizers, the Federation is
the ringleader of an alliance composed of itself, the Grange, the
National Council of Farmer Co-operatives, the Co-operative Milk
Producers' Federation, and other big producers' organizations
representing the "top tier" of farmers, processors and distributors.
[A. Whitney Griswold in *Farming and Democracy*]

These farmers have a very different interest from that of
the poorer farmers and look on federal policy with a very
critical eye if it seems to threaten the present set-up. Thus,
we are told, the Farm Bureau regarded with grave suspicion
the work of the Farm Security Administration, which was
attempting to salvage the marginal farmers, ruined in the
depression, and desperately clinging to their often uneco-
nomic farms.

Even though it has helped with cash and encouragement in
thousands of pitiable cases of human misery, it is accused of har-

boring outright "reds" as well as "pinks" on its ample pay roll.
. . . Farmers are the main accusers, especially the American Farm
Bureau Federation, which represents the American equivalent of
the "landed aristocracy" and the most powerful of the farmers'
general pressure groups. [W. M. Kiplinger in *Washington Is
Like That*]

The interests of farmers vary a great deal and produce
opposing patterns of political demand accordingly. A congressional subcommittee touring New England, finds that
the farmers of that region have very different interests from
the grain farmers of the Middle West who want a high price
for what they sell to New England farmers, grain stuffs, for
instance. Dairy farmers have much the same interest, na-
tionally speaking, in all parts of the country. But in state
politics, dairy farmers want, and sometimes succeed in getting, legislation that sets up a kind of tariff wall to protect
their rights in *their* "milk shed," not only from Canadian
exports, but from exports from Wisconsin. Then, since
American farmers are human, they are, to a certain, though
not to a crippling extent, embarrassed by the contrast between the legend and the facts. They see themselves as the
sole, independent, self-supporting element in the American
community. They may have to accept what they think their
due from the federal government, but they would rather
(especially if they belong to the "landed aristocracy" of the
Farm Bureau) do without open handouts. For the farmers,
the "country's pride," have a pretty clear picture of what a
farmer should be—and they don't quite fit into the picture. . . . It would be unkind to dismiss this moral malaise
as mere humbug. But it would be idle, too, to expect the
farmer, at any rate the average farmer, not a member of
highly disciplined religious groups like the Mormons or
Mennonites, to prefer his lonely mountain top of independence to what he thinks is his due. Frederick the Great said
of the scruples that afflicted the Empress Maria Theresia
[of Austria] about taking part in the partition of Poland:
"She wept and took." So does the American farmer.

It is possible, but no more than possible, that the farmer may politically as well as economically, be pricing himself out of the market. The great urban majority that cannot pay for the foodstuffs whose price it keeps up through the taxes it pays, is becoming restive. Fashions and fads in food, the terror of calories that affects the American woman, the decline of the hard manual labor that provoked the appetites of the men, changes in world production, all have upset the American farm pattern and law and lobbies, in the long run, must be adjusted to the facts. But it may be quite a long run, at any rate as long as the American people believe with the "Country Life Commission" appointed by Theodore Roosevelt, that one aim, perhaps the main aim of American policy, should be "to preserve a race of men in the open country that, in the future as in the past, will be the stay and strength of the nation in time of war, and its guiding and controlling spirit in time of peace." [Griswold, *Farming and Democracy*]

THE AMERICAN FARMER . . . OUR FIRST "HYBRID" [7]

You naturally think of our fabulously efficient system of agricultural production as uniquely American. And it is. But when you take a look back at its historic origins, you may see that what's unique about our agricultural system is the hybrid vigor from its highly varied origins.

For example, the American tradition of independent owner-operator farming came to America as part of the cultural baggage of the first English colonists. They were not especially conscious of their "yeoman farmer" heritage, because the small, independent land-holding farmer had been increasingly squeezed out and down-graded by expanding British landholders. But the first settlers quickly reverted

[7] Edited version of article by Roe C. Black, executive editor of *Farm Journal*. *Farm Journal*. 100:24–6+. F. '76. Reprinted by permission of the author who supplied text.

to type when they had to wrest their living from the wilderness.

In fact, it is not too far fetched to say that the Jamestown settlers were the first to try "corporate farming" and declare it a failure. The Virginians, along with the Plymouth colonists, recognized early the essential role of individual enterprise in agricultural success.

Captain John Smith decribes the failure of company farming for the London company which colonized Jamestown:

> When our people were fed out of the common store and labored jointly together, glad was he who could slip from his labor or slumber over his tasks. The most honest among them would hardly take so much true pains in a week as now for themselves they will do in a day. We reaped not so much corn from the labors of thirty as now three or four do provide for themselves.

William Bradford, governor of the Plymouth Colony in Massachusetts, found the value of family incentives early. And the system he devised of assigning "to every family a parcel of land, according to the proportion of their number" was essentially the same democratic system of land distribution that was used throughout New England. Over two hundred years later it was transformed into a national homestead policy.

"This had very good success," writes the governor, "for it made all hands industrious so as much corn was planted than otherwise would have been by any means the governor or any other could use. The women now went willingly to the field, and took their little ones with them to set corn." Before, they would have pleaded weakness and inability, and to have compelled them would have been thought a great tyranny and oppression, he added.

The British

The early British farmers—English, Scots and Scotch-Irish—were not content to be mere subsistence farmers and certainly not peasants tied to the soil alone. They had their "trading shoes" on right from the start. As early as 1624, the Pilgrims had learned their corn-farming lessons from Squanto so well that they produced a surplus boatload of corn. They sent it north to the Kennebec River where it was exchanged for seven hundred pounds of beaver and other furs.

By the time of the Revolution, American export trade in grain, livestock, flaxseed, indigo, tobacco and other farm commodities was so important it became a major cause of the war for independence. Big planters and small farmers wanted more freedom to trade without British restrictions which were getting tougher.

Our Scotch-Irish ancestors are probably responsible for another trait that has become typical of American farmers— a willingness, even eagerness to pioneer and develop new farms, new methods, new ideas.

In the early 1600s, the English had encouraged these tough Scotch Presbyterians to settle North Ireland and hold it against the Irish who had been pushed out of the area ruthlessly. Hold it and settle it they did, building a solid farm economy that eventually threatened the English who had put them there. By the early 1700s, the English cracked down on their trade, stepped up persecution of the Presbyterian leaders, and doubled tenant rents, in many cases. The first Scotch-Irish to come here accepted an invitation by William Penn, and 200,000 more followed. They came through Philadelphia, filled the outer fringe of the central Pennsylvania frontier, and flowed down the Great Wagon Road through the Shenandoah Valley and on into North and South Carolina and Georgia to occupy the first "West."

The Scotch-Irish were used to fighting for their farms in Northern Ireland, and they were among the staunchest fighters in the French and Indian War in the mid-eighteenth century and the American Revolution.

J. C. Ramsey, a Southern farmer of the early 1800s tells how deep this pioneering trait was imbedded in his father who was like many in his time. He had taken his family from Georgia to Mississippi in six successive moves, cutting and burning brush, chopping down trees, developing new cabin homes, and working up pens for livestock at each new location.

He appeared [Ramsey wrote of his father] to take up the idea that improving new places and selling them out to other new-comers was better for him; more money in it; than to remain in one place and make larger improvements.

In other words, pioneering was his way of life, as it was for generations of Americans.

This "British element"—English, Scotch, Scotch-Irish and Welsh—makes up about one third of the . . . white popula-tion of the United States—and that probably goes for farm-ers, too. The next most important element of national origin is German. Historian A. B. Faust estimates 25 percent of our background is German, though it may be higher than that among farmers.

The Germans

The German reputation for success in farming and live-stock production was the reason German immigrants were invited in the first place by William Penn in 1683. He wanted to populate Pennsylvania with industrious people.

University of California historian Theodore Saloutos points out that

the Germans, unlike English, Scotch-Irish and Welsh who were more interested in large landholdings and commercial farming, embraced farming as a way of life instead of just another way of making a living.

Like the Scotch-Irish, the Germans were frontiersmen but with one important difference. The Scotch-Irish surrendered some of their good land. The Germans retained theirs, permitted their sons to move West, and formed compact social and economic units to help insure their permanence on the land. Unlike other frontier farmers, the Germans tried to become self-sufficient.

In 1789 Benjamin Rush wrote:

A German farm may be distinguished from the farms of other citizens . . . by the superior size of their barns, the height of their inclosures (fences), the extent of their orchards, the fertility of their fields, the luxuriance of their meadows, and the general appearance of plenty and neatness in everything that belongs to them.

Geographer Walter Kollmorgen writes:

Not only did the Pennsylvania German adopt new kinds of crops and better stock, he also perfected and popularized certain seeds, crops and foods . . . He pioneered in the rotation and diversification of crops and in providing good shelter for stock. Conservative as he was in some matters, he was, nevertheless, a progressive farmer.

And these characteristics were and are visible wherever farmers of German descent settled—mainly in a straight line west of Pennsylvania.

You can credit our German heritage with much of the inventiveness American farmers have always been known for. Two early examples are the Conestoga wagon and the long rifle developed in the eighteenth century in Pennsylvania Dutch country. The first was the famous vehicle that rolled the pioneers West to the Pacific. The second was the weapon that the pioneer farmer needed to shoot his dinner, defend his cabin and family and later provide the winning handicap in the Revolution. Unbelievably accurate, the rifle was the American "secret weapon." It helped whip British regulars who had to be massed in rank to get fire power from inaccurate muskets.

The Russian Germans

Another group of Germans made a unique contribution to American agriculture—the Russian Germans who migrated to the Ukraine in the late eighteenth century in return for religious privileges, then migrated to America in the nineteenth century when those privileges were taken away.

They came in large numbers starting in 1873, bringing with them the hard red winter wheat that had been their staple commodity in Russia, dry farming know-how such as deep plowing, and thorough surface cultivation needed in the Plains.

The Scandinavians

If the spirit of independence in farming, political democracy and cooperative action needed a shot in the arm in nineteenth century America, the next major group of immigrants—the Scandinavians—provided it in large measure. "The United States had great appeal for the dispossessed sons and daughters of free farmers and tenant classes of Sweden from the 1850s on through the 1880s," says Saloutos. In the home country, land was handed down by the laws of entail and primogeniture, so whole farms passed to the oldest son or a family member who could buy him out. There were plenty of young people attracted to American free land. And there was plenty of it in areas like the upper Midwest where the climate was familiar to the northern Europeans who came here.

The Swedes, unlike farmers of other nationalities, often plunged straight into the wilderness or wandered into the small prairies in small groups, choosing the most inaccessible places instead of near rivers and lakes that offered easy communication [Saloutos writes].

"There would be a great void in the Northwest today could a million citizens of Swedish descent be removed from this territory," boasted one proud Swede in 1921. "But for them, large tracts would be primeval forests, and what are now the most fertile fields of their great region would still be waste land."

The Norwegians were individualists, more so than the other Scandinavians and the Germans. Their experience under the constitution of Norway had given them individual rights. They had taken part in labor disputes and strikes, become acquainted with socialism, demanded a greater voice in government and formed cooperatives.

Eastern Europeans

Often poor, land hungry and willing to match anyone in physical labor, the immigrant farmers from Eastern Europe—Poles, Czechs and Finns—earned their way into American farming the hard way. In the upper Midwest, they often worked in lumber camps to earn enough to farm, then settled on cutover, poorer land that the affluent passed up.

But they persisted and succeeded like millions before them. In her novel, Willa Cather describes the success so hard won by "My Antonia" and her husband on the dry, tough plains of Nebraska. Cuzak, Antonia's immigrant Bohemian husband, sums up the struggle:

It was a pretty hard job, breaking up this place and making the first crops grow [he said pushing back his hat and scratching his grizzled hair]. Sometimes I git awful sore on this place and want to quit, but my wife she always say we better stick it out. The babies come along pretty fast, so it look like it be hard to move anyhow. I guess she was right, all right. We got this place clear now. We pay only $20 an acre then, and I been offered $100.

Other Immigrants

Other immigrant groups brought special knowhow. The Swiss in Wisconsin originated a thriving dairy industry. The Italians in California and New Jersey applied their savvy with fruits and vegetables. The Japanese contributed in intensive agriculture such as irrigation farming. African blacks supplied generations of labor to the opening and development of southern agriculture.

Blacks made another very significant contribution to American agriculture. They brought sorghum seeds with them from Africa in slave ships, according to John T. Schlebecker in his new agricultural history, *Whereby We Thrive*. The varieties ranged from sorgo or sugar sorghum to milo, kaffir grass, broom grass and over one thousand other types. Potential development is still immense.

French immigrants put a unique stamp on the South.

Descendants of Acadian French forced into exile from farms in Nova Scotia became the backbone of the rich cattle, rice, and sugar cane industries of the Gulf Coast from Mississippi to Beaumont, Texas.

A different kind of misfortune—the great potato famine—resulted in a substantial contribution to American agriculture from the Irish. Although only about one in ten Irish immigrants chose farming after they arrived here, they came in such numbers that their impact has been important. Entire farm communities such as that around Emmetsburg, Iowa, still identify with and take pride in their Irish heritage.

Above all, we must recognize the Spanish contribution to agriculture, a contribution all out of proportion to the number of farmers and stockmen who can claim Spanish roots. Spaniards introduced to North America not only the horse but also nearly every citrus fruit, a number of deciduous fruits, many types of vegetables, spices, sugar cane, and hundreds of flowers.

U.S. AGRIBUSINESS AND
AGRICULTURAL TRENDS [8]

The American farmer earned the approval of Alexis de Tocqueville, the premier observer of democracy in America, by carrying the "businesslike qualities of Americans into agriculture." As a business, however, farming has proved perilous for the individual farmer. The dominant pattern in US agriculture has been for production to exceed demand so that farming has undergone a prolonged process of attrition, forcing a great migration from the farm. The result has been a continuous growth in the average size of farms as part of a trend in the whole food industry toward

[8] Article by John Walsh, staff writer. *Science*. 188:531–4. My. 9, '75. Copyright 1975 by the American Association for the Advancement of Science. Reprinted by permission.

concentration and integration. While growth in productive efficiency has been remarkable, the social costs incurred have been great.

The intractable, long-term trend in American agriculture, as one recent study of resource allocation and farming efficiency puts it, has been the "tendency to expand production to the point at which product prices fail to cover investment and expenditures in producing farm products."

By this analysis, US agriculture has been characterized by overcapitalization and overallocation of manpower. The outcome has been a relatively cheap food supply for the population at large. This boost to the general standard of living, however, has been subsidized by expensive government crop support and other aid programs and by low income for the farmers themselves.

In economists' terms, the farmer is locked into atomistic competition in which the individual producer has no influence on the price of what he sells. In addition he lacks adequate knowledge to adjust his production plans, and hence he has remained at the mercy of the market as well as of the weather. Government programs designed to protect the family farm against the worst effects of price fluctuations were established during the 1930s; but the competitive advantage of larger, more highly capitalized farming units has continued to increase, and the mortality rate of smaller units has remained high. In three decades the number of farms has steadily dropped, and the average size of farms has increased.

The farmer, whether a major or marginal operator, is part of a total agricultural system which has changed drastically in this century and continues to change at a rapid rate. Large corporations now dominate some sectors of this system, and the term *agribusiness* is used to denote large, industrial-type operations along the commercial food chain. Agribusiness has a growing band of critics who use the term pejoratively. A nonnormative definition in a recently released report on the changing structure of agribusiness, issued by the US Chamber of Commerce, says agribusiness refers to "commercial farms, input industries (those which provide the farm machinery, pesticides, fertilizers, etc.) and marketing and processing firms which contribute to the total food sector." It is primarily the agribusiness trends which, along with market fluctuations, are determining the character of farm operations.

The term *corporate farming* summons up images of big business owning and cultivating limitless acreages. For a number of reasons, big corporations have, for the most part, avoided the production phase of agriculture and concentrated on providing inputs—machinery, fertilizers, pesticides, animal biologicals—and on outputs, the processing and marketing of food products.

The simple explanation is that the profit is not, in general, to be found in the production end of the business. A major deterrent to corporation farming is the price of prime agricultural land, which has doubled and even trebled in the past few years. Corporations are reluctant to tie up the necessary amounts of capital in land and machinery on which the record shows that the return on investment is likely to be low—perhaps 3 to 4 percent a year if things go reasonably well. Furthermore, farming lends itself poorly to centralized management. Decisions on when to prepare the soil, plant, cultivate, and harvest require training, experience, and a close knowledge of local conditions; and they cannot be made from corporate headquarters. Hired managers may not be disposed to make the exertions—the eighteen-hour day is a necessity in some circumstances on a farm —or to minimize costs as the owner-operator is. And a significant number of big production ventures by large corporations have ended in enormously costly failures.

Large-scale farming by corporations is by no means an inconsequential factor in food production, but such operations are concentrated in particular crops and regions. Feedlots—on which livestock are fattened, and often then slaughtered, and processed—and vegetable and fruit growing processing operations seem to lend themselves best to successful big-corporation efforts.

Landholding and Labor Patterns Influenced by History

Historical circumstances that influence landholding and labor patterns appear to be a factor. It seems no accident that corporations are particularly active in California, Texas, and Florida. Large landholdings in California and the Southwest originated with Spanish land grants. In the South, large holdings can be traced to the plantation system and reclaimed land.

The extent of the incursion of big corporations into production is in dispute. Data from the last census indicate that big corporations are responsible for perhaps 3 percent of total producton. Other estimates, taking into account the activities of corporations classified as nonfarm operations, put the total at 5 to 8 percent. While the total share of production is still modest, corporations dominate certain activities such as producing broilers, seeds, and vegetables for processing. The importance of corporations in the production of citrus fruits, feed cattle, turkeys, and eggs is growing.

Corporations will venture into production to exploit new technology. The broiler industry, for instance, was developed and is dominated by industry. Some corporations have been attracted to farming by the prospect of later selling farm land profitably for other uses. In the Southwest, ranching and oil production have been combined, and a similar pattern is emerging in Wyoming and other northern plains states that have coal deposits suitable for strip-mining. In the Southeast, particularly, large tracts of marsh and coastal land have been reclaimed for agriculture. Typically, the aim is to create an integrated enterprise with feed grains grown to fatten hogs and cattle raised on the same lands. Such projects in North Carolina alone will cover hundreds of thousands of acres and are being developed by Japanese and Italian as well as American corporate owners.

The family farm, however, rather surprisingly remains the basic production unit in the system, although the term *family farm* must be carefully defined. About 16 percent of the farms in the United States account for some 70 percent of cash receipts. Therefore, it is fair to inquire what is meant by a farm. To be so categorized by government data-gatherers, the farm must yield $2,500 a year in cash sales. Obviously a family with a farm income at that level would need income from other sources to survive. And many farmers do rely on off-farm jobs for themselves, their wives, or children to supplement the farming income. Studies of farm income, conducted by land-grant institutions, showed that, around 1970, a farmer needed, on the average, sales of $20,000 a year or more over a long period to ensure earnings sufficient to cover costs. Data from the last census showed that only about 550,000 farms out of the total 2.7 million had more than $20,000 in sales. It was this roughly 20 percent of all farms, however, that produced about three quarters of all food and fiber.

The optimal mix of land, capital, and labor for a profitable operation differs by crop and region. In the Corn Belt, one man, equipped with the proper machinery, can handle virtually all the work necessary to farm 600 to 800 acres of corn. He will need help from his family or one or two hired workers only at the busiest times. If the farmer fattens hogs or cattle in the same region, not so much land is required. Hogs, for example, can be profitably raised on 300 to 400 acres of land planted in corn or soybeans for feed. In the last few years, farmers with smaller acreages or poorer land could cover costs because of higher market prices, but downward trends in prices are squeezing such farmers.

In the Corn Belt, the typical ownership patterns are the father-son combination, the partnership, or the family corporation. These family corporations are often larger operations and are formed because they provide advantages in dealing with tax and inheritance problems. Of the approximately 1.2 percent of commercial farms that are incorporated in the United States, about 90 percent are family corporations.

Successful farms generally follow the trend toward specialization observable in large, corporate farms. The farm concentrates on one crop or one type of livestock and maximizes output by the use of specialized machinery and by developing a particular expertise. Within one enterprise, for example, a father may concentrate on managing crops and his son, on livestock. Unless a farmer can attain an efficient-sized operation he is likely to fail. In dairy farming, which is now highly mechanized, a ratio of forty cows per worker is regarded as economic. The old pattern of the farm with a herd of eighteen or twenty milking cows is no longer viable.

For successful farmers, the problem of passing their farms on to the next generation has been compounded by the rise in land costs. A six-hundred-acre farm in a prime agricultural area may now be valued at $1 million or more. Each new generation has to be refinanced, and the costs of inheritance taxes and settlement of an estate create a heavy financial burden for the heir to assume. It is even harder for someone starting from scratch to enter farming and build a successful operation.

Informed observers, nevertheless, tend to see present patterns persisting. In . . . 1974 two Economic Research Service economists of the United States Department of Agriculture suggested the following:

A continuation of present trends where a relatively few large farms will dominate the farm production sector appears the most likely scenario to develop. A few large farms will account for most of the farm output, but a large number of small farms will continue whose operators will use most of their labor and secure most of their income from off-farm sources. The present financial institutions financing farm production would be relegated to a lesser role than in today's market, but still would provide a large amount of borrowed funds. Equity financing through securities sold in capital markets would probably become an important source of funds.

A major expansion of corporation ownership, involving growth of a cadre of hired managers and workers and the development of a new rural social structure, was accounted less likely as was a return to dominance of the small family farm.

Evolving Relationship of Corporations to Individual Farmers

Perhaps more significant currently than the role of agribusiness in food production is the evolving relationship of corporations to individual farmers. Increasingly, farmers are making contracts with grain companies or food processors to take their crops at negotiated prices. This protects the farmer against a downward slide of the market after harvest and allows him to plan and manage his operations more effectively, but it also prevents his reaping the rewards when prices rise above the level in his contract.

In some sectors, the process of integration has gone much further. In the broiler industry, the farmer, typically, owns the land and buildings, while the corporation owns the chickens and provides inputs such as feed and pharmaceuticals and makes decisions that used to be the province of the poultryman. It is the broiler industry which is as close to applying the mass production techniques of industry as any sector of agriculture. And the corporations have developed field staffs expert at chicken raising and adept at management.

Other agribusinesses have expanded customer services to an extent that is markedly modifying the technology transfer process in agriculture. A new commercial chain is developing, closely linking the manufacturers of inputs with distributors, dealers, and farmers.

In recent years, farmers have shown a partiality for "one stop" service by a dealer who can sell and service machinery and supply fertilizer, pesticides, fuel, and animal biologicals according to the farmer's special needs. This trend has contributed to the decline of the small town in rural areas by putting individual tractor dealers and Main Street merchants out of business. The big dealer does more than operate an agricultural supermarket. He is likely, for example, to prescribe and mix fertilizer to meet a customer's needs and even apply it for the farmer. Dealers increasingly have become major credit sources for their customers, and have assumed functions traditionally provided by local banks. Often the dealer or distributor becomes a major owner and leaser of agricultural land.

Farmers have come to depend heavily on the suppliers for information and expertise, and large input manufacturers have moved to meet this demand by hiring and training field representatives to fill a role once exclusively that of the agricultural extension service agent. A . . . 1974 report, *Agricultural Production Efficiency,* from the National Academy of Sciences (NAS) indicated that studies of the source of information used by farmers showed increasing reliance on commercial sources.

In many cases the county agent is no longer the sole source of information leading to technological innovation in farming, but rather often acts as an intermediary. Through their dealers and representatives, corporations now effectively mix information and sales pitches mostly by the means of farmers' meetings, which can range from church suppers to sophisticated seminars.

This revolution in American agriculture that has brought major advances in productive efficiency has not been viewed with unanimous approval. Residual reflexes from the nineteenth century populist resentment of the banks, the railroads, and commodity speculators are now directed at agribusiness. But a new strain of Naderite and consumer-protection protest is gathering strength. In part the protest is directed at the "disenfranchisement" of the small farmer and exploitation of migrant and other farm workers. The critics also charge that trends in agriculture created by an alliance between agribusiness and the land-grant establishment often work to the disadvantage of both the consumer and the small farmer.

The argument is made in extended form in the book *Hard Tomatoes, Hard Times,* published [in 1972] by the Agribusiness Accountability Project. The main theme of the critique is that crops these days are bred for machines not for the consumer and that the land-grant R & D establishment, at the expense of the taxpayer, has "developed a total mechanization system for agribusiness that has abandoned the independent farmer. . . ." The result has been a succession of changes for the worse in rural America. The agricultural research establishment has come under criticism in recent years from peer scientists who have deprecated the quality of research and of research leadership.

The Small Landholder Fights Back

Public sympathy for the cause of the family farm is almost instinctive in the United States, tracing back to Jefferson's eulogizing of the small landholder as the chief repository of virtue in the republic. The principal organized effort to advance the interests of the small operator is conducted through the cooperative movement and the National Farmer Organization (NFO). Begun as a protest movement in the 1950s, NFO evolved into a national membership organization providing alternative policies to those of the National Farm Bureau Federation, the largest of farmer organizations and said to be dominated by members from among the more prosperous sector of farming.

The NFO's major initiative has been to organize collective bargaining on crop sales to affect prices favorably for its members. It sponsors legislation intended to become a Family Farm Act, which would extend antitrust legislation to prohibit big nonfarm businesses from entering farming if their assets or sales were above certain levels.

The questions raised by structural changes in agriculture are complex and have received little effective attention when farm legislation has been debated. Nor does the subject appear to be getting serious attention now that it has been found necessary to enact "emergency" farm legislation.

Farm policy in the United States has been shaped by a contest and compromise between those who believe in allowing the free play of market forces to determine prices and those who favor government intervention to protect the farmer against disaster in the marketplace. Federal action has been guided by the United States Department of Agriculture's ill-defined policy of seeking to ensure adequate food supplies at reasonable prices and a pragmatic aim of preventing the ruin of the majority of efficient farmers.

The years 1972 to 1974 were, by and large, boom years for US farmers, and some observers believed that a basic shift in circumstances might permit farmers in this country to flourish at near-full production in the future. As other articles in this section indicate, however, the conditions that produced the boom may be of short duration. Recent declines in crop prices suggest that the old pattern is reasserting itself, and, although bad weather here and abroad could reverse the decline, the familiar uncertainties of the marketplace appear to be reviving. Farm policy is once more being seriously debated in Washington—this time, whether fully recognized or not, with vital international as well as national implications.

Agriculture Secretary Earl L. Butz is a proponent of the free-market approach, and, in 1973, an Administration measure was passed replacing the established crop support and acreage restriction programs with a more flexible income-support system. If the market price of basic crops fell below "target price" levels, the farmer is guaranteed payments to make up the difference.

The program was passed at a time when market prices were well above existing support levels. Now, prices have been falling and farm income levels declining, while the prices that the farmer pays for energy, farm machinery, and other production requirements are still rising. And the current congressional reflex is to legislate increases in target prices to compensate.

So far, the discussion in Washington has been conducted mainly along conventional lines, concentrating on the renewed shortfall between prices and costs. The experience of 1972 to 1974, which was highly unsettling to consumers at home and abroad and, ultimately, to farmers, seems to have had little impact. The question of creating a world food reserve as an adequate cushion against poor harvests has not been directly addressed, nor has the possibility of long-term changes in climatological pattern been taken into account. So, for American farmers, who are in an uncertain business, it appears to be business as usual.

III. SHIFTING PATTERNS IN RURAL AREAS

EDITORS' INTRODUCTION

This final section of the book deals with change in rural areas. William N. Ellis, an independent consultant on state-federal relations, discusses the new ruralism and the possibility of the beginning of a postindustrial age. An article from *Organic Gardening and Farming* follows, with pointers for successful homesteading.

Among the middle class, the ideal of living on and working the land continues to exert its pull (although frequently accompanied by the sad realization that some other income-producing source is needed to support a farm), whereas the situation of the rural poor—small farmers, migrant workers, and other marginal groups—has continued to deteriorate. A New York *Times* article by Jon Nordheimer discusses the new face of rural poverty and the need for a national program to sustain small farms.

The concluding selections are first-hand accounts of life on, or under, the land, from Studs Terkel's book *Working*. The last of these, "Second Chance," was chosen as a companion piece to the first article in this volume, by Alexis de Tocqueville. The theme is the peculiarly American phenomenon of constantly moving on to new lands, unlike the European or Asian heritage of staying in one place.

THE NEW RURALISM: THE POST-INDUSTRIAL AGE IS UPON US [1]

The US Bureau of Census population projections for 1970–1973 [see Table p 158] indicate that the future may be

[1] Article by William N. Ellis, independent consultant on state-federal relations. *Futurist.* 9:202–4. Ag. '75. Reprinted by permission of *The Futurist*, published by the World Future Society, P.O. Box 30369 (Bethesda), Washington, D.C. 20014.

closer than we think. They also show that those most concerned with projecting the future are the least prepared for it. These population estimates show that people are leaving the urban centers in droves and moving to the remote, rural and least developed parts of our country, a startling reversal of the trend of urban growth and rural decay which has been the basis of policy planning since 1880.

Since the 1970 census, seventeen states have shifted from large out-migration to substantial in-migration. All of these (Maine, Minnesota, Iowa, North and South Dakota, Nebraska, North and South Carolina, Kentucky, Tennessee, Alabama, Arkansas, Montana, Idaho, Wyoming, New Mexico, Utah) are rural states. The most dramatic shift was New Mexico, which lost 14.7 people for each one thousand during the 1960-70 decade but gained 13.4 per thousand in the three-year period of 1970–73. Overall these rural states had a net in-migration of 478,000 in this three-year period.

The reversed trend becomes even more startling when one notes that the twenty most rapidly growing states today, with the exceptions of Florida and Delaware, are rural. Many of these saw the turnaround a number of years ago. Arizona, for example, has long been growing, but in this period led all the rest with an in-migration of 35 per thousand, followed closely by Florida with 33.5 per thousand. Nevada, which took in 43 per thousand for the decade of the fifties and 40.9 per thousand during the sixties, decreased its growth rate to 22.5 per thousand. New Hampshire continued its rapid rise from 2.2 to 10.8 to 14.6 in these same three periods, and Colorado's rate of in-migration shot from 11.6 for the 1960–70 period to 21.3 for the 1970–73 period.

Out-Migration Increases in Urban States

On the other side of the coin, the more urban states saw an increase in out-migration taking place between 1970 and 1973. About half of the 2.402 million migrants moving into rural states came from the urban areas; the rest were from overseas. Between 1970 and 1973, fifteen states had a civilian out-migration totaling 1.198 million (nearly 400,000 per year). Five of these states (Mississippi, Alabama, Louisiana, Missouri, Kansas) are rural states with long histories of out-migration; but, in every one the rate of out-migration decreased markedly in this three-year period. Seven urban states (Connecticut, New York, Washington, Ohio, Indiana, Illinois, Michigan) have shown a strong tendency to increase their out-migration since the 1970 census. For example, 346,000 people left New York State alone in these three years. In addition to those states currently showing net out-migrations, at least three urban states (California, Maryland, New Jersey) appear to be trending toward out-migration. California, for example, was attracting people at a net rate of 26 per thousand in the fifties, but has declined steadily to a net intake of only 2.1 per thousand in the latest census estimates; a continued decrease would mean an annual outflow from California of some 200,000 by 1980.

If current trends continue, twelve urban states will be sending 800,000 people annually to the rural areas—more than double the current rate—by 1980.

A closer look at the areas of in-migration shows little correlation between these statistics and the usual population magnets. The Ozarks, Appalachia, the Upper Peninsula of Michigan, the Rocky Mountains, and Northern New England, to which people are moving, have few of the economic and cultural amenities which Americans of the past have held in high esteem. Within New England, for example, the two most remote, poorly serviced and economically depressed counties, Aroostook and Washington in Maine, are witnessing the greatest turnaround in migration. Both counties shifted from having substantial out-migration to the in-migration column; meanwhile their unemployment rate was over 11 percent and their $2,092 average per capita income was 59 percent below the $3,558 national average.

MIGRATION PATTERNS

Net Migration (per thousand initial population)

	1970-73	1960-70	1950-60	1940-50
Rural States				
Maine	4.7	–7.4	–7.6	–3.2
Minnesota	0.4	–0.7	–3.4	–6.4
Iowa	3.6	–6.9	–9.4	–8.0
North Dakota	3.2	–16.1	–18.6	–20.9
South Dakota	1.8	–14.8	–15.7	–13.1
Nebraska	5.9	–5.3	–9.2	–10.8
North Carolina	2.3	–2.1	–8.4	–7.5
South Carolina	5.2	–6.5	–11.1	–12.9
Kentucky	4.2	–5.2	–14.2	–13.8
Tennessee	8.1	–1.3	–8.7	–5.0
Alabama	10.3	–7.4	–12.9	–12.9
Arkansas	11.0	–4.1	–25.7	–23.9
Montana	4.2	–9.0	–4.3	–7.4
Idaho	12.8	–6.5	–7.0	–5.3
Wyoming	9.7	–12.6	–7.1	–0.4
New Mexico	13.4	–14.7	7.4	3.0
Utah	9.5	–1.3	1.3	1.6
Urban States				
Connecticut	–1.4	8.1	11.0	6.4
New York	–4.6	–0.3	1.4	2.0
Washington	–5.0	8.4	3.6	20.4
Ohio	–5.4	–1.3	5.0	3.5
Indiana	–1.1	–0.4	1.5	2.8
Illinois	–3.7	–0.4	1.4	0.9
Michigan	–3.1	0.3	2.4	6.2
California	2.1	12.6	26.0	32.6
Maryland	3.9	11.7	12.8	13.8
New Jersey	2.8	7.7	11.3	6.8

U.S. Bureau of Census statistics reveal a significant shift in migration patterns in the period 1970-1973. 17 rural states gained people, while many urban states either lost people or gained them at a much slower rate.

Affluent May Be Moving to Rural States

Careful statistics do not yet tell us who is leaving the urban-industrial centers or why they are leaving, but some facts and speculations may provide clues. Traffic statistics of the Allied Van Lines identifying "magnet" states for household moves using Allied's services are heavily skewed toward the more affluent elements of America. They indicate that rural states have become magnets for the more affluent. From 1969 through 1971 Vermont was the leading state, with three families moving in for each one moving out. Maine, Alabama, Alaska, and Tennessee were among the magnet states for this period. In 1972 and 1973 Florida took over the lead, but Colorado, Alabama, Arizona, New Hampshire, Georgia, Nevada, North Carolina, and Oregon attracted considerably more households than left the state.

Less solid evidence suggests that the rural areas are becoming havens for youth escaping the urban-industrial syndrome; young professionals exchanging material gain for the psychic income of less pressured lifestyles; middle-career entrepreneurs investing their savings in more personalized enterprises; and early retirees seeking to make more meaningful contributions in their later years. If these groups predominate, major social and political shifts may be expected in the next decade. Colorado, for example, a state with high in-migration for over a decade, has seen a "young outsider" successfully challenge a "native son" Coloradan for a Senate seat. The epithets of "eastern establishment" or "carpetbagger" had little effect on the state because of its strong minority of affluent new citizens.

The economic impact will be no less severe. Rural land values are already feeling the pressures as acres of farm and forest land are being bought up by affluent new citizens. Major effects may also result from multiple small investments of the in-migrants. Ten thousand migrants investing $50,000 each in small businesses would provide new capital totaling $500 million, which would have considerable eco-

nomic impact on any of the now economically deprived
rural states.

New National Policies May Be Needed

The abrupt reversal of trends which have held for over
one hundred years puts in serious doubt many national policies and future projections. For example, it has been generally accepted that by 1990, 80 percent of the US population
will be concentrated in four urban-industrial complexes,
one reaching from Atlanta to Boston, another along the
California coast, a third in the Dallas-Houston region and
the other from Chicago to New York. This scenario has
fostered policies to train rural youth for urban jobs, to concentrate transportation funds on city problems and to aim
the national research and development effort at the problems of big business; in short, to continue in the directions
set by the industrial revolution. The flight from the cities
suggests all this may be in error; the industrial revolution
may be coming to an end and a postindustrial age may be at
hand.

The industrial age grew because agricultural and cottage
industries could not meet the expanding needs of man. The
postindustrial age is coming because man's current needs
cannot be met by the city and the factory. The industrial
age gave man his material needs and it used gratification of
material needs to create ever greater material wants. The
past few decades in America have shown the awakening of
new needs—the psychic needs of man. "Quality of life," "belonging," "independence," "beauty," and "individual potential" are among the watchwords of our new age. The
postindustrial age will aim at meeting man's psychic needs.

The city grew as a tool of the industrial revolution. To
meet man's material needs labor, resources and power had
to be concentrated. The limits of transportation and communications gave no choice but the creation of large centralized urban industrial complexes. Rural areas were
needed only for the supply of raw materials. Those who

were left behind in rural areas imitated the amenities of city life to the greatest extent possible.

New Ruralism May Mark Beginning of Postindustrial Age

A new ruralism is becoming the tool of the postindustrial age. Wilderness sports have a new popular appeal; forest retreats are replacing city conference centers for industrial meetings; pastoral settings are being chosen for rehabilitation services for heart attack patients, alcoholics, drug addicts and others suffering from the pressures of modern industrialism. To the greatest extent possible those left behind in city and suburb are reaching for the benefits of rural living.

As more Americans recognize the false trap of materialism, the flow to rural areas will accelerate. Demands for rural technologies will remove what barriers still exist for the urban outflow. Industry will decentralize under pressure from employees for more fulfilling work relationships. The shibboleth of economic gain through economies of large scale will be replaced by the doctrine of psychic gain through enterprises of small scale.

A full scenario for the new ruralism has not yet been worked out. It will, no doubt, create new problems as well as new benefits. But migration statistics clearly indicate that the policies, plans and projections of the past are no longer valid, and it behooves federal, state and local governments to bring their programs in closer harmony with the emerging America.

THE KEYS TO HOMESTEADING SUCCESS [2]

You wouldn't believe the people who move back into the mountains to get away from big cities [a state agricultural official was telling me in a concerned voice]. They are unbelievably naïve. The scenic beauty of the mountains attracts them, I guess. They don't understand that those hollows and mountainsides are some

[2] Article by Gene Logsdon, staff writer. *Organic Gardening and Farming.* 22:128–31. N. '75. Reprinted by permission.

of the worst places anywhere to try to produce your own food. One family let its livestock literally starve to death. Their garden was just weeds. They would have starved to death themselves without welfare.

You can find back-to-the-land horror stories like that, but for every one of them you can also find two examples of success. Many homesteaders have graduated magna cum laude from city to country or from small garden to small farm—even with the odds against them. They'll be the first to tell you it isn't easy and they are more than willing to talk about their mistakes and what it takes to make a happy homestead.

What kind of person makes a good homesteader? There are exceptions to everything, but after visiting hundreds of country dwellers, I can describe rather precisely the model most likely to make it.

1. The traditional family group—husband, wife and average of two children—most often succeeds. Average age of the married partners is about thirty-five. But married couples over fifty-five, though a minority of the total homesteading families, have the best rate of success. Solo homesteaders and other social groups, including communes, have a high casualty rate.

2. Both partners possess enthusiasm for the venture.

3. This enthusiasm is evidenced by an absorbing interest in nature and the out-of-doors that is both scientific and artistic in bent. But the interest is not primarily bookish, effete or "poetic." Thoreaus (as Thoreau himself proved) make poor homesteaders.

4. The successful homesteader derives mental and physical satisfaction from monotonous, often uncomfortable physical labor most people find distasteful.

5. At least one of the partners, and often both, will be of a pragmatic and no-nonsense turn of mind, coldly plotting the move to the country with all the deliberateness of a banker deciding whether to make a loan or not. The cal-

culating may span a decade or more of careful preparation—sometimes a whole working lifetime before the move is put into effect.

6. The successful homesteader is not unsuccessful in the city—by which I mean he does not come to the country fleeing failure. Those who believe that a change in environment will somehow automatically improve their financial condition or their intrafamily relationships are doomed to disappointment.

7. The successful homesteader does not move to the country *primarily* to escape city problems. If that is his prime or only motive, then he finds soon enough that pollution, crime, high costs and lack of privacy must also be dealt with in the country. It is rather difficult to escape the human race anymore.

8. The successful homesteader is lower-to-middle class. He is rarely rich. When young people desiring the "good country life" finally realize that goal demands hard work and painstaking financial planning, they throw up their hands and dismiss homesteading as a "rich kid's fad." Not so. The rich will give homesteading a roll or two in the clover and that's all. Afterwards they "keep" the country place for parading friends on weekends and during summer months.

9. Homesteaders are invariably shy. Crowds they avoid like the plague. The public eye makes them nervous. They'd rather sweat a week in a hayfield than give a five-minute speech. They dislike telephone conversations. They are reluctant party-goers. Talked into taking a trip, they can't wait to get back home. *Homebody* is the best synonym in the dictionary for the successful homesteader.

10. Last and most important, the homesteaders most likely to last are those who have had experience living in the country, then moved to the city, and then moved back out again. Only a person who has actually experienced both life styles can make a fair choice between them. Unless he has a poor memory, he moves back to the country fully

aware of the advantages and disadvantages. He also knows
—or should know—enough about farming and gardening to
avoid amateurish mistakes.

This type of homesteader *knows how,* and because he
does, you seldom think of him as a homesteader. He doesn't
match the image. He doesn't seem to be *struggling* enough.
Paul and Anne Downs of Louisville, Kentucky, make a good
example. A quick glance and you'd say the Downs family
was typical suburbanite—good job, nice house, etc. If you
asked them, they might say the same thing. But look again.

Behind the Downs' home, Paul grows about five acres of
fruits and vegetables. His gardens reflect professionalism at
every turn. No place have I seen healthier, more productive
vegetables, grapes, strawberries and apples. Anne keeps the
larder stocked with food—canned, frozen, dried, fresh.

Their day may begin like any of their neighbors, when
Paul goes off to work (air traffic controller at the Louisville
airport). But when the neighbors come home to nest or tend
their yardwork, Downs sheds the disguises of his job world,
climbs on his tractor, and becomes what he really is; a small
homesteader-farmer and carpenter. (He built an addition to
his home any professional carpenter would be proud of.) "I
don't know why I work so hard out here," Paul likes to say
with a grin. "It's a bad habit I can't get rid of." But he and
Anne are really dead serious about their avocation. They
find in it not only good food and some to sell, but a certain
satisfaction that fulfills their sense of artistry and their sense
of independence. "It's a way to preserve family life, too,"
says Paul. "There are just too many outside activities pulling
the family apart."

Downs' excellent gardens are not by chance. Paul is a
farm boy and learned from his father a deft knowledge of
truck farming. After a stint in Cincinnati, he and Anne returned to the Louisville area and bought a chunk of his
father's farm then being broken up for development. Downs
has had many chances to take higher-salaried positions at

airports in larger cities, but he has opted to remain in what I call the Almost-Perfect Homestead Situation—partaking of the best in both city and country life.

But you don't have to stop planning a homesteading venture just because you don't have a previous experience. If you don't get in a hurry, you can make the switch successfully by learning as you go, as thousands of our readers attest. You need to follow only two basic rules:

1. Make your move only with the assurance that you have another source of income. "A country place is supposed to be a *life*," observes homesteader-writer Jim Ritchie in Missouri. "A harsh fact of life is that it's darned hard to earn a livelihood on a few acres in the country without a skill, trade or craft of some sort." And trades—carpenter, stone mason, electrician, plumber, mechanic, etc.—are far more reliable than crafts. Bank on a craft only if you have *proved* you can make it produce adequate income. Don't be like the dreamer-writers who think that once they get out in the woods someplace, the words will flow in torrents upon their paper, all of them salable. Never.

2. Undertake all projects, including the move itself, *gradually.* "Rent a house first," says Indiana homesteader Jean Harper. "Find out if you're cut out for the 'good life.' "

Chuck and Linda Brayton in Hadley, Massachusetts, believe strongly in the rental route to homesteading.

If we would have had the down payment [says Linda], we'd probably have gone ahead and bought a farm even though our local Farmer's Home Administration officer said it would be financial suicide. We know now that he was correct and our inability to buy was probably a blessing in disguise.

The Braytons had, in their words, "almost nothing going for them." Less than an acre went with the house which they rented, and the only barn was a small chicken coop. They found they could rent hay ground and barn and learn how to grow feed for livestock without incurring serious financial risk. Now they are taking one more step: they will rent ground to try to grow a crop of grain to sell.

The gradual approach is the wisest course for any homestead project. One homesteader (Kansas) read an article in *Organic Gardening and Farming* on the profits possible in raising blackberries. He purchased and planted over $500 worth of plants, which due to his inexperience and lack of time to care for properly, have been an almost total failure. A much wiser homesteader (Ohio) read the same article, then purchased half-a-dozen plants of six kinds of bramble fruit. These he has tended assiduously. The varieties that do well in his soil, he will gradually increase vegetatively at no cost but his time, until he has a large planting capable of producing $500 in a few years, rather than losing $500.

Rick and Jan Jones of Spokane, Washington, have been homesteading only a few months, but already they understand that haste makes waste. By their own admission, they've made mistakes by ignoring good advice. "Every book you read will tell you not to try to do everything you've ever dreamed of all at once," says Jan good-naturedly, "but we didn't read that part very carefully." The young homesteaders first had all kinds of trouble with their goats, including white muscle disease, and had to sell them. "Someday, I hope to try again," says Jan, "but not until I learn quite a bit more about them."

About a week later, the Joneses went to an auction to buy some pigs—and came home with a nine-month-old heifer calf instead. Not a fence on the farm held her. "Five days later we located her two miles away at a neighbor's place," says Jim.

Linda Brayton can tell the same kind of not-so-hilarious stories.

We went to an auction "just to watch" and came home with two piglets. We were even more ill-prepared for them than Chuck's bull calves, which we had purchased just days before. We had to cart the squealing pigs home in the back seat of the car, then in the dead of night, make some hasty renovations to the chicken coop—which had already been renovated for the calves.

We worked industriously at fencing a place in which our bouncing baby bulls could romp, and at building an indestructible pen for the pigs. No sooner had we turned the calves loose and stood back to watch their antics with doting pride than one of the precocious little fellows took a tremendous leap right over the five-foot fence.

The drawback to our indestructible pigpen was not so quickly discovered. Only after a rainy spell did we find out that, while it makes sense to sink planks into the ground to prevent the pigs from tunneling their way to the outside world, the planks, resting on hardpan, effectively blocked all drainage. Neither we nor the pigs appreciated a wall-to-wall swimming pool.

But even the experienced homesteader can make mistakes if he gets in a hurry. When he started his orchard, Paul Downs had a chance to move trees from an established orchard in the path of a housing development.

Seemed like a good idea. We had the farm equipment to do the job and no other cost but our labor. We knew how to transplant larger trees, and it would mean an instant orchard instead of waiting for years. So we did it, against the advice of an orchardist I respected. He said we'd be bringing diseases and bugs to our new orchard site, and that the trees—even if they lived— would not do well and would fail just about the time young nursery trees would have been coming on strong. He was right. I would have been better off to put out a new block of trees and forget the instant orchard.

Linda Brayton sums it up. "Taking one step at a time means a chance to learn without risking heavy financial loss. You gain confidence, too, as you learn. And you get to know farmer neighbors who can be overwhelmingly generous in their help and advice. Dull and tedious though it may sound, breaking into small farming business slowly but surely is good strategy."

AMERICA'S RURAL POOR:
THE PICTURE IS CHANGING [3]

Rural poverty in the United States is not what it used to be. Over the last fifteen years, the number of people classified as poor living in the countryside has declined 56 percent, largely because of migration to the cities and economic diversification.

A notable example of the change is West Virginia, long associated with chronically depressed conditions. West Virginia is still a poor state by most national standards, but the resurgence of the coal industry has created thousands of new jobs and growing incomes in the coal fields of Appalachia. West Virginia's unemployment rate is lower than the national average, which has been rising.

In 1959 there were 21.6 million Americans in nonmetropolitan areas subsisting on incomes beneath the poverty level; today the figure is 9.3 million. Poverty has always been a relative, inexact term in the United States. The federal government sets a poverty level by several criteria. In 1974 the income figure was $5,038 for a nonfarm family of four.

It generally is accepted that it is easier for the rural poor to live on meager incomes—especially in milder climates—than people in urban ghettos. However, access to public assistance programs, health centers and educational services is not as readily available in rural areas as in the cities.

Traditional areas of rural poverty continue to be the spawning grounds of the poor: economically depressed farms and woodlands, marginal mill towns, Indian reservations, the small town barrios of the Southwest, and, of course, the South.

A major factor in the change in rural poverty has been the migration to the cities, particularly the industrial centers of the North. In 1959, the majority of poor people,

[3] Article by Jon Nordheimer, staff reporter. New York *Times*. sec IV, p 2. Ag. 17, '75. © 1975 by The New York Times Company. Reprinted by permission.

56 percent of the total 38.7 million at the time, lived in rural America; today 60 percent of the 23 million live in metropolitan areas.

The Return of the Natives

The South, long the nation's poorhouse of rural blacks and whites, cleared an aggregate of 9 million persons from the poverty list of sixteen states in this period. Although the region continues to account for two out of every three impoverished persons living in nonmetropolitan areas, the thrust of economic improvements in the South holds the potential for even greater gains for this segment of the population. This promise is seen in the return to the South of natives, both black and white, who were the economic exiles from southern agriculture over the past two decades.

By 1970, one out of every eight white southern migrants had returned home to resettle. The corresponding figure for former black migrants was one out of twenty-five, but it at least contains the seeds of an important demographic shift. The return of the native black to the South with skills that he acquired in the North has equipped him for a new role.

Economic diversification has been the key to improving rural income, not only in the South but in the rest of the nation. The average farm operator in the United States today is only a part-time farmer. Studies show that most farm families now derive a substantial amount of income from nonfarm labor, an improvement correlated to the liberation of the farm wife from purely domestic chores to take employment off the farm.

The rural blacks in the South represent the most intractable core of poverty in the nation. About 2.3 million blacks remain locked in penury. They have been by-passed by industrialization, which has occurred chiefly outside the regions of the old plantation economy system.

There are 3.2 million poor whites in the South, and they are the ones who have benefited more from the industrialization. Coupled with the dynamics of the new interstate highway system, the expansion of industry has created a web of manufacturing plants and distribution service centers in once-remote locations.

Impact on Migrant Workers

The migrant farm worker is another member of the rural poverty scene who has barely survived the changes of the 1960s. When growers were forced to make reforms in housing, wages and working conditions of the migrants, many opted to mechanize instead, which in the long run would be less expensive than the human labor force.

Many migrants went to the cities, taking low-paying jobs or welfare; those that remain are still impoverished.

One problem of the rural poor has been that the programs designed to attack poverty have been the product of urban legislators confronted with the conditions of the city. Professor Ray Marshall of the Center for the Study of Human Resources at the University of Texas, among others, feels there is an opportunity to promote rural development at this time because of the increasing number of urban Americans who would like to live in a rural environment but cannot because of the paucity of employment opportunities.

Professor Marshall argues that a national program to sustain small farms, improve health care and education, and provide the groundwork for increased cultural amenities, could benefit not only those living in the countryside but also create an attraction for city-dwellers eager to escape urban pressures.

WORKING THE LAND [4]

Pierce Walker

An autumn evening in a southern Indiana farmhouse. The city, Evansville, industrial and distending, is hardly fifteen miles away—and coming on fast.

It's a modern, well-appointed house. A grandfather's clock, tick-tocking, is the one memento of a "country" past. His father and his grandfather worked this land. "My father was born on the same spot this house is sittin'. And I was born here. We tore the old house down."

His wife, who has a job in the city, and their fourteen-year-old daughter live with him. His older child, a son, is elsewhere. Though he has a few head of beef cattle, soy beans and corn are his source of income. He describes himself as "a poor farmer."

I farm about five hundred acres. I own in the neighborhood of two hundred. The rest of it I sharecrop. I give the owners two fifths and I keep three fifths. They're absentee. One would be a doctor. And a bricklayer. One would be a contractor widow. (Glances toward his wife) What would you call Roger? An aeronautical engineer. I guess all of 'em have inherited from their parents. They hold it for an investment. If I owned a lot of farm land myself, if I had that much money, I don't think I'd be farming it. I'd let somebody else worry with it.

For a farmer, the return on your investment is so small now that it isn't really worthwhile. A younger person cannot start farming unless they have help from the father or somebody. Cause you have to be almost able to retire a rich man to start out. The only way the farmers are making it today is the ones in business keep getting bigger, to kinda offset the acreage, the margin income. I don't know what's

[4] From *Working: People Talk About What They Do All Day, and How They Feel About What They Do*, by Studs Terkel, reporter and interviewer. Pantheon Books. '74. p 3–19. Copyright © 1972, 1974 by Studs Terkel. Reprinted by permission of Pantheon Books, a division of Random House, Inc.

gonna happen in the future. I'm afraid it's gonna get rough in time to come.

Your cities are moving out, taking the farm land. If you want to stay in the farming business, it's best not to be too close to the city. But if you're thinking of disposing of your farm in a few years, why then it's an advantage, 'cause it'll be worth a lot more.

I don't see how I'll keep the thing goin'. As I get older and want to slow down . . . Well, that's one way of looking at it, retirement. It's either gritting it out or selling. It seems nowadays a lot of 'em do retire and rent it out to a neighbor or somebody. The end of the day, the older you get, the tireder you get.

City people, they think you're well off. When they drive by, I hear a lot of comments, 'cause most of my friends are city people. They drive by and see a big tractor and things settin' down. They envy me, but they don't know what's behind all that.

Farming, it's such a gamble. The weather and the prices and everything that goes with it. You don't have too many good days. It scares when you see how many working days you actually have. You have so many days to get the crop planted and the same in the fall to harvest it. They have this all figured down to the weather and it's just a few days. You try to beat the weather. It tenses you up. Whether we needed rain or we didn't need rain, it affects you in different ways. I have seen a time when you're glad to hear the thunder and lightning. Then again, I've wished I didn't hear it. (Laughs.)

Mrs. Walker interjects: "In his busy season, every morning when we get up the radio goes on right away so we can get the weather report. About ten to six every morning. We just eagerly listen to this report. In the summer when he isn't too busy or like in the winter, we never pay too much attention to it. Otherwise, we watch it close."

Weather will make ya or break ya. The crops have to have enough moisture. If they don't have enough, they hurt. If you have too much, it hurts. You take it like you git. There's nothing you can do about it. You just don't think too much about it. My wife says it doesn't bother me too much. Of course, you still worry. . . .

I don't believe farmers have as much ulcers as business people 'cause their life isn't quite as fast. But I'll say there will be more as times goes on. 'Cause farming is changing more. It's more a business now. It's getting to be a big business. It's not the labor any more, it's the management end of it.

Your day doesn't end. A farmer can't do like, say, a doctor—go out of town for the weekend. He has to stay with it. That's just one of the things you have to learn to live with. I'd say a majority of the time a farmer, when he comes in at night and goes to bed, he's tired enough he's not gonna have trouble sleepin'. Of course, he'll get wore down.

He touches a weary cadence as he recounts a twelve-plus-hour workday in the fall: up at six (an earlier rising in the spring, four thirty-five) . . . "haul my grain to the elevator in town, which takes about an hour and a half . . . combine about three or four loads a day . . . there's headlights on the combine, so if I start a load, I'll finish it even though it's after dark . . . that'll run from fifteen hundred to two thousand bushel . . . five hundred bushels a truckload . . . first thing next morning, I'll take the load to town . . ."

In the winter he "loafs," helping his wife with her housework, preparing the machinery for spring, planning the fertilizer program, and "a lot of book work," getting all the records up to date for "tax time."

We'll soon be storing the fall harvest. Machinery and a lot of equipment and everything ready to go when the crops mature. That's the big problem: machinery. Combine, you're speaking of twenty thousand dollars. And the eight-row planter for the spring, that's expensive. It's such a large investment for what small return you really get out of it. You won't use it but a month or two out of the year.

My father-in-law helps me an awful lot in the spring and a little in the fall. He drives the tractor for me. My daughter, she drives a tractor when school is out. When I was home there on the farm, there was five children, three boys, and we were on an eighty-acre farm. It took all of us, my father and three boys. You can see the difference machinery plays in it.

The number of farmers are getting less every day and just seems like it's getting worse every year. The younger ones aren't taking over. The majority of the people originated from the farm years ago. But it's been so long ago that the young ones now don't realize anything about the farm. What goes with it or anything like that. The gamble that the farmer takes.

The city people, when they go to the grocery store and the price of meat is raised, they jump up and down. They don't realize what all is behind that. They're thinking of their own self. They don't want to put up that extra money —which I don't blame them either. The same way when I go to buy a piece of equipment. I go jump up and down.

Break the dollar down for food and the farmer's down at the bottom of the list. He's got the most invested of all but he's the smallest percentage-wise out of the food dollar. The processors, it seems like that's the big end of it. The ladies like to buy this ready-prepared and frozen and all that, and that costs 'em.

And chemicals in farming, it's getting to be quite expensive. It seems as though we can't farm without it. They're tryin' to outlaw a lot of 'em, but I don't know. From my end of it, I'd hate to be without 'em. Seems as though if we didn't have chemicals, we wouldn't have crops. It seems like the bugs and the weeds would just about take care of 'em if we didn't have the chemicals. But I don't know . . . on the other end, either . . . whether it's good for our country or not.

What do you call these—organic farming? They have a lot of good points, but I never did see a large organic farm. They're just more or less small operators. I don't think you can do it on a large scale enough to be feeding a nation. You can see many small organic farms. They used to call 'em truck farmers. They had routes to town and deliver produce and like that. He more or less retailed his product to individual homes. He just couldn't get big enough, just like everybody else.

They're using airplanes more all the time. We had our corn sprayed this year by a plane—for blight. You hire a plane, he furnishes the material, and he does it for so much an acre. We had it sprayed twice—with fungicide.

When you get a good crop, that's more or less your reward. If you weren't proud of your work, you wouldn't have no place on the farm. 'Cause you don't work by the hour. And you put in a lot of hours, I tell ya. You wouldn't stay out here till dark and after if you were punchin' a clock. If you didn't like your work and have pride in it, you wouldn't do that.

You're driving a tractor all day long, you don't talk to anyone. You think over a lot of things in your mind, good and bad. You're thinking of a new piece of equipment or renting more land or buying or how you gonna get through the day. I can spend all day in the field by myself and I've never been lonesome. Sometimes I think it's nice to get out by yourself.

The grass is greener on the other side of the fence, they say. When I got out of high school I worked one summer in a factory in Evansville. I didn't like it. I've always been glad I worked that one summer. I know what it is to work in a factory for a little while. The money part of it's good, but the atmosphere, confined. The air and everything like that. I wasn't used to a smelly factory. They have a certain odor, you don't have it out in the field.

I might say I've been real lucky in farming. My wife has helped me an awful lot. She's worked ever since we've been married. My girl, she likes it and loves to get out on the tractor. Our boy really worked. He liked the farm and worked from the time he was old enough until he left. He graduated from Purdue last spring. From observing him from the time he grew up, I would say he'd make a good farmer. He's in Georgia now. He's in management training. He realized he could make more money in some other position than he can farming. I hope he isn't putting money ahead of what he really wants to do. He says he likes what he's doin', so. . . .

It seems like if they once get out and go to college, there's very few of 'em do come back. They realize that as far as the future and the money could be made from farming, it just wasn't there. So that was one thing that turned his mind away from it. Of course, he can always change. I'm hoping. . . .

I do believe farmers are going to have to band together a little bit more than they have in the past. Whether it'll be through a cooperative or a union, I can't say. The trouble is they're too much individual for the rest of the country nowadays. You're bucking against the organized country, it seems like. And the farmers aren't organized, it seems like.

The big complaint you hear is that when you take your product to the market, you take what they give you. And when you go buy on the other end, you pay what they say. So you're at their mercy on both ends, more or less.

I don't like to—farmers really don't want to, deep in their hearts—but when it gets to a certain point, there's no alternative. 'Cause when a person gets desperate or is about to lose his farm, he'll do about anything he wouldn't do otherwise.

I hate to look at it that way, if the farmer is part of an organization, that would take all the—I wouldn't say enjoyment, no—but it'd be just like any other business. When you all had to sell at a certain time and all that went with it. But I believe it is going to come to that.

POSTSCRIPT: *"The family farm has never been stronger than it is now, and it has never been better serviced by the Department of Agriculture."—Earl L. Butz, Secretary of Agriculture, in the keynote speech at the 51st National 4-H Congress* (Chicago Sun-Times, *November 27, 1972).*

Roberto Acuna

I walked out of the fields two years ago. I saw the need to change the California feudal system, to change the lives of farm workers, to make these huge corporations feel they're not above anybody. I am thirty-four years old and I try to organize for the United Farm Workers of America.

His hands are calloused and each of his thumbnails is singularly cut. "If you're picking lettuce, the thumbnails fall off 'cause they're banged on the box. Your hands get swollen. You can't slow down because the foreman sees you're so many boxes behind and you'd better get on. But people would help each other. If you're feeling bad that day, somebody who's feeling pretty good would help. Any people that are suffering have to stick together, whether they like it or not, whether they be black, brown, or pink."

According to Mom, I was born on a cotton sack out in the fields, 'cause she had no money to go to the hospital. When I was a child, we used to migrate from California to Arizona and back and forth. The things I saw shaped my life. I remember when we used to go out and pick carrots and onions, the whole family. We tried to scratch a livin' out of the ground. I saw my parents cry out in despair, even though we had the whole family working. At the time, they were paying sixty-two and a half cents an hour. The average income must have been fifteen hundred dollars, maybe two thousand. Today, because of our struggles, the pay is up to two dollars an hour. Yet we know that is not enough.

This was supplemented by child labor. During those years, the growers used to have a Pick-Your-Harvest Week.

They would get all the migrant kids out of school and have 'em out there pickin' the crops at peak harvest time. A child was off that week and when he went back to school, he got a little gold star. They would make it seem like something civic to do.

We'd pick everything: lettuce, carrots, onions, cucumbers, cauliflower, broccoli, tomatoes—all the salads you could make out of vegetables, we picked 'em. Citrus fruits, watermelons—you name it. We'd be in Salinas about four months. From there we'd go down into the Imperial Valley. From there we'd go to picking citrus. It was like a cycle. We'd follow the seasons.

After my dad died, my mom would come home and she'd go into her tent and I would go into ours. We'd roughhouse and everything and then we'd go into the tent where Mom was sleeping and I'd see her crying. When I asked her why she was crying she never gave me an answer. All she said was things would get better. She retired a beaten old lady with a lot of dignity. That day she thought would be better never came for her.

"One time, my mom was in bad need of money, so she got a part-time evening job in a restaurant. I'd be helping her. All the growers would come in and they'd be laughing, making nasty remarks, and make passes at her. I used to go out there and kick 'em and my mom told me to leave 'em alone, she could handle 'em. But they would embarrass her and she would cry.

"My mom was a very proud woman. She brought us up without any help from nobody. She kept the family strong. They say that a family that prays together stays together. I say that a family that works together stays together—because of the suffering. My mom couldn't speak English too good. Or much Spanish, for that matter. She wasn't educated. But she knew some prayers and she used to make us say them. That's another thing: when I see the many things in this world and this country, I could tear the churches apart. I

*never saw a priest out in the fields trying to help people.
Maybe in these later years they're doing it. But it's always
the church taking from the people.*

*"We were once asked by the church to bring vegetables
to make it a successful bazaar. After we got the stuff there,
the only people havin' a good time were the rich people
because they were the only ones that were buyin' the
stuff . . ."*

I'd go barefoot to school. The bad thing was they used
to laugh at us, the Anglo kids. They would laugh because
we'd bring tortillas and frijoles to lunch. They would have
their nice little compact lunch boxes with cold milk in their
thermos and they'd laugh at us because all we had was dried
tortillas. Not only would they laugh at us, but the kids
would pick fights. My older brother used to do most of the
fighting for us and he'd come home with black eyes all the
time.

What really hurt is when we had to go on welfare. Nobody knows the erosion of man's dignity. They used to have
a label of canned goods that said, "U.S. Commodities. Not
to be sold or exchanged." Nobody knows how proud it is
to feel when you bought canned goods with your own
money.

*"I wanted to be accepted. It must have been in sixth
grade. It was just before the Fourth of July. They were trying out students for this patriotic play. I wanted to do Abe
Lincoln, so I learned the Gettysburg Address inside and out.
I'd be out in the fields pickin' the crops and I'd be memo-
rizin'. I was the only one who didn't have to read the part,
'cause I learned it. The part was given to a girl who was a
grower's daughter. She had to read it out of a book, but
they said she had better diction. I was very disappointed. I
quit about eighth grade.*

*"Any time anybody'd talk to me about politics, about
civil rights, I would ignore it. It's a very degrading thing
because you can't express yourself. They wanted us to speak*

English in the school classes. We'd put out a real effort. I would get into a lot of fights because I spoke Spanish and they couldn't understand it. I was punished. I was kept after school for not speaking English."

We used to have our own tents on the truck. Most migrants would live in the tents that were already there in the fields, put up by the company. We got one for ourselves, secondhand, but it was ours. Anglos used to laugh at us. "Here comes the carnival," they'd say. We couldn't keep our clothes clean, we couldn't keep nothing clean, because we'd go by the dirt roads and the dust. We'd stay outside the town.

I never did want to go to town because it was a very bad thing for me. We used to go to the small stores, even though we got clipped more. If we went to the other stores, they would laugh at us. They would always point at us with a finger. We'd go to town maybe every two weeks to get what we needed. Everybody would walk in a bunch. We were afraid. (Laughs.) We sang to keep our spirits up. We joked about our poverty. This one guy would say, "When I get to be rich, I'm gonna marry an Anglo woman, so I can be accepted into society." The other guy would say, "When I get rich I'm gonna marry a Mexican woman, so I can go to that Anglo society of yours and see them hang you for marrying an Anglo." Our world was around the fields.

I started picking crops when I was eight. I couldn't do much, but every little bit counts. Every time I would get behind on my chores, I would get a carrot thrown at me by my parents. I would daydream: If I were a millionaire, I would buy all these ranches and give them back to the people. I would picture my mom living in one area all the time and being admired by all the people in the community. All of a sudden I'd be rudely awaken by a broken carrot in my back. That would bust your whole dream apart and you'd work for a while and come back to daydreaming.

We used to work early, about four o'clock in the morning. We'd pick the harvest until about six. Then we'd run home and get into our supposedly clean clothes and run all the way to school because we'd be late. By the time we got to school, we'd be all tuckered out. Around maybe eleven o'clock, we'd be dozing off. Our teachers would send notes to the house telling Mom that we were inattentive. The only thing I'd make fairly good grades on was spelling. I couldn't do anything else. Many times we never did our homework, because we were out in the fields. The teachers couldn't understand that. I would get whacked there also.

School would end maybe four o'clock. We'd rush home again, change clothes, go back to work until seven, seven thirty at night. That's not counting the weekends. On Saturday and Sunday, we'd be there from four thirty in the morning until about seven thirty in the evening. This is where we made the money, those two days. We all worked.

I would carry boxes for my mom to pack the carrots in. I would pull the carrots out and she would sort them into different sizes. I would get water for her to drink. When you're picking tomatoes, the boxes are heavy. They weigh about thirty pounds. They're dropped very hard on the trucks so they have to be sturdy.

The hardest work would be thinning and hoeing with a short-handled hoe. The fields would be about a half a mile long. You would be bending and stooping all day. Sometimes you would have hard ground and by the time you got home, your hands would be full of calluses. And you'd have a backache. Sometimes I wouldn't have dinner or anything. I'd just go home and fall asleep and wake up just in time to go out to the fields again.

I remember when we just got into California from Arizona to pick up the carrot harvest. It was very cold and very windy out in the fields. We just had a little old blanket for the four of us kids in the tent. We were freezin' our tail off. So I stole two brand-new blankets that belonged to a grower. When we got under those blankets it was nice and comfortable. Somebody saw me. The next morning the grower told my mom he'd turn us in unless we gave him back his blankets—sterilized. So my mom and I and my kid brother went to the river and cut some wood and made a fire and boiled the water and she scrubbed the blankets. She hung them out to dry, ironed them, and sent them back to the grower. We got a spanking for that.

I remember this labor camp that was run by the city. It was a POW camp for German soldiers. They put families in there and it would have barbed wire all around it. If you were out after ten o'clock at night, you couldn't get back in until the next day at four in the morning. We didn't know the rules. Nobody told us. We went to visit some relatives. We got back at about ten thirty and they wouldn't let us in. So we slept in the pickup outside the gate. In the morning, they let us in, we had a fast breakfast and went back to work in the fields.

The grower would keep the families apart, hoping they'd fight against each other. He'd have three or four camps and he'd have the people over here pitted against the people over there. For jobs. He'd give the best crops to the people he thought were the fastest workers. This way he kept us going harder and harder, competing.

When I was sixteen, I had my first taste as a foreman. Handling braceros, aliens, that came from Mexico to work. They'd bring these people to work over here and then send them back to Mexico after the season was over. My job was to make sure they did a good job and pushin' 'em even harder. I was a company man, yes. My parents needed money and I wanted to make sure they were proud of me. A foreman is recognized. I was very naïve. Even though I was pushing the workers, I knew their problems. They didn't know how to write, so I would write letters home for them. I would take 'em to town, buy their clothes, outside of the company stores. They had paid me $1.10 an hour. The farm workers' wage was raised to eighty-two and a half cents. But even the braceros were making more money than me, because they were working piecework. I asked for more money. The manager said, "If you don't like it, you can quit." I quit and joined the Marine Corps.

"I joined the Marine Corps at seventeen. I was very mixed up. I wanted to become a first-class citizen. I wanted to be accepted and I was very proud of my uniform. My mom didn't want to sign the papers, but she knew I had to better myself and maybe I'd get an education in the services.

"I did many jobs. I took a civil service exam and was very proud when I passed. Most of the others were college kids. There were only three Chicanos in the group of sixty. I got a job as a correctional officer in a state prison. I quit after eight months because I couldn't take the misery I saw. They wanted me to use a rubber hose on some of the prisoners—mostly Chicanos and blacks. I couldn't do it. They called me chicken-livered because I didn't want to hit nobody. They constantly harassed me after that. I didn't quit because I was afraid of them but because they were trying to make me into a mean man. I couldn't see it. This was Soledad State Prison."

I began to see how everything was so wrong. When growers can have an intricate watering system to irrigate their crops but they can't have running water inside the houses of workers. Veterinarians tend to the needs of domestic animals but they can't have medical care for the workers. They can have land subsidies for the growers but they can't have adequate unemployment compensation for the workers. They treat him like a farm implement. In fact, they treat their implements better and their domestic animals better. They have heat and insulated barns for the animals but the workers live in beat-up shacks with no heat at all.

Illness in the fields is 120 percent higher than the average rate for industry. It's mostly back trouble, rheumatism and arthritis, because the damp weather and the cold. Stoop labor is very hard on a person. Tuberculosis is high. And now because of the pesticides, we have many respiratory diseases.

The University of California at Davis has government experiments with pesticides and chemicals. To get a bigger crop each year. They haven't any regard as to what safety precautions are needed. In 1964 or '65, an airplane was spraying these chemicals on the fields. Spraying rigs they're called. Flying low, the wheels got tangled on the fence wire. The pilot got up, dusted himself off, and got a drink of water. He died of convulsions. The ambulance attendants got violently sick because of the pesticides he had on his person. A little girl was playing around a sprayer. She stuck her tongue on it. She died instantly.

These pesticides affect the farm worker through the lungs. He breathes it in. He gets no compensation. All they do is say he's sick. They don't investigate the cause.

There were times when I felt I couldn't take it any more. It was 105 in the shade and I'd see endless rows of lettuce and I felt my back hurting. . . . I felt the frustration of not being able to get out of the fields. I was getting ready to jump any foreman who looked at me cross-eyed. But until two years ago, my world was still very small.

I would read all these things in the papers about Cesar Chavez and I would denounce him because I still had that thing about becoming a first-class patriotic citizen. In Mexicali they would pass out leaflets and I would throw 'em away. I never participated. The grape boycott didn't affect me much because I was in lettuce. It wasn't until Chavez came to Salinas, where I was working in the fields, that I saw what a beautiful man he was. I went to this rally, I still intended to stay with the company. But something—I don't know—I was close to the workers. They couldn't speak English and wanted me to be their spokesman in favor of going on strike. I don't know—I just got caught up with it all, the beautiful feeling of solidarity.

You'd see the people on the picket lines at four in the

morning, at the camp fires, heating up beans and coffee and tortillas. It gave me a sense of belonging. These were my own people and they wanted change. I knew this is what I was looking for. I just didn't know it before.

My mom had always wanted me to better myself. I wanted to better myself because of her. Now when the strikes started, I told her I was going to join the union and the whole movement. I told her I was going to work without pay. She said she was proud of me. (His eyes glisten. A long, long pause.) See, I told her I wanted to be with my people. If I were a company man, nobody would like me any more. I had to belong to somebody and this was it right here. She said, "I pushed you in your early years to try to better yourself and get a social position. But I see that's not the answer. I know I'll be proud of you."

All kinds of people are farm workers, not just Chicanos. Filipinos started the strike. We have Puerto Ricans and Appalachians too, Arabs, some Japanese, some Chinese. At one time they used us against each other. But now they can't and they're scared, the growers. They can organize conglomerates. Yet when we try organization to better our lives, they are afraid. Suffering people never dreamed it could be different. Cesar Chavez tells them this and they grasp the idea—and this is what scares the growers.

Now the machines are coming in. It takes skill to operate them. But anybody can be taught. We feel migrant workers should be given the chance. They got one for grapes. They got one for lettuce. They have cotton machines that took jobs away from thousands of farm workers. The people wind up in the ghettos of the city, their culture, their families, their unity destroyed.

We're trying to stipulate it in our contract that the company will not use any machinery without the consent of the farm workers. So we can make sure the people being replaced by the machines will know how to operate the machines.

Working in the fields is not in itself a degrading job.

It's hard, but if you're given regular hours, better pay, decent housing, unemployment and medical compensation, pension plans—we have a very relaxed way of living. But the growers don't recognize us as persons. That's the worst thing, the way they treat you. Like we have no brains. Now we see they have no brains. They have only a wallet in their head. The more you squeeze it, the more they cry out.

If we had proper compensation we wouldn't have to be working seventeen hours a day and following the crops. We could stay in one area and it would give us roots. Being a migrant, it tears the family apart. You get in debt. You leave the area penniless. The children are the ones hurt the most. They go to school three months in one place and then on to another. No sooner do they make friends, they are uprooted again. Right here, your childhood is taken away. So when they grow up, they're looking for this childhood they have lost.

If people could see—in the winter, ice on the fields. We'd be on our knees all day long. We'd build fires and warm up real fast and go back onto the ice. We'd be picking watermelons in 105 degrees all day long. When people have melons or cucumber or carrots or lettuce, they don't know how they got on their table and the consequences to the people who picked it. If I had enough money, I would take busloads of people out to the fields and into the labor camps. Then they'd know how that fine salad got on their table.

Aunt Katherine Haynes

A worked-out mining town in eastern Kentucky, Blackey. It is near the Virginia border. The Cumberlands are in view; is it fog, smoke, or a heavy dust that causes them to appear more distant than they really are? The people of the town, population 350—the young have gone—are, many of them, of Revolutionary War stock. Most are on welfare.

Along the superhighway, cutting through the mountains, gangs of men are casually engaged in road repair. All day trucks and half-trucks rumble by, kicking up clouds of coughing dust. During the trip to Blackey, there were glimpses of deep "hollers" and shacks; and an occasional person. Half-hidden by the mountain greenery were the ubiquitous small mountains of slag.

We're behind the mountains, deep in the hollow, Bull Creek. It's a long, winding, tortuous dirt road, some seven miles from Blackey.

Aunt Katherine Haynes is seventy-four. She lives by herself in a cottage, on the rocks, at the foot of the mountains. It is surrounded by caterpillar tractors and bulldozers. On the wall, among olden photographs, is the legend: God Bless Our Home. It is a spare place, singularly neat: a folded umbrella in one corner, a homemade broom in another; an ancient brass bedstead is the one conspicuous piece of furniture.

She recalls the hollow of her small girlhood: "The road, a horse could travel it, but that was all. No cars, no wagons, or no nothin' back then. Then they went to have wagons and kinda widened the road up. Each man used to work six days a year, free labor. On the roads. If he wasn't out on the days the others was, why they laid him off a bigger piece to finish and he had to do that. That was the law. They always done it in the fall of the year.

"In the fall of the year, it's the prettiest place you've ever seen. When the leaves is colored . . . it's beautiful to see the hills when it's colored like that, brown and red and green and yeller. The pines always looks green and if the rest is all colored, the pines shows up.

"There was more big trees then, but the fields were cleaned up and tended. You can see there's nothin' cleaned up any more, 'cause I ain't able to do it. . . ."

Housework and farmin' is all I done, never worked at nothin' else. Eighteen hours out of every twenty-four. Out-of-doors and then in the house at night. I have worked out in the fodder field and carry it in some time after dark. We'd stack it by moonlight. Never got much rest on what little time I was in bed. (Laughs.)

You usually didn't get much rest on Sunday, had to cook for ten children on Sunday. I've raised ten and I had eleven. Three meals a day I cooked on Sunday. I got so I couldn't cook like I used to. I used to be out here just runnin' and cookin' those meals in a few minutes and fillin' the table full. But my mind just jumps from here to there and I can't do that no more. Just hard work, that's all I ever knowed.

I can run circles around every girl I've got in the house today. I'm awful thankful for it, but I won't hold up much longer. I'm gittin' down. Used to be I could stand and split wood all day long, but now I go out there and split a little while and it hurts the back of my legs to stoop over. But I done awful well I think.

I just don't know. I was just raised an old hillbilly and I'll die one. Radio, it's sittin' up there, but I cain't hear too good. Don't have a television. I say there's too much foolishness on for me to watch. I hear a little about Vietnam. And I study a lot about it. But I have enough worry on my mind without listenin' to that to worry more about. What was to be would be. No, I don't guess I have a grandson in Vietnam now. Terry's boy, I actually don't know if he's out of Vietnam or not.

They wasn't much to think on when you didn't have no education. I didn't get half through the third reader, so I've got no education at all. Only five months of school. I just quit out until we got the fodder saved. Then it got so cold, I couldn't go back. I'm just a flat old hillbilly. That's the only way I know to talk and the only way I'll ever try to talk.

There was fifteen in the family and we were raised in a log house. There wasn't a window in the house. If we seen how to do anything in the winter, we done it by firelight. There wasn't even a kerosene lamp. We had to keep the door open regardless of how cold it was. If you needed to work at somethin' we either done it by the light of the fire in the grate or opened the door. We always kept a good fire.

That was the way I learnt to write. I'd get me a piece of clay dirt out of the cracks and write on the side of the log house. I couldn't write a line when I was goin' to school. Now that's the truth.

Joe and Susie Haynes

Aunt Katherine's nephew and his wife. On this morning, a piece of sun peers over the Cumberlands. "That's young white oaks up there a growin'," he says. "They'll be there till the strip and auger [a variation of strip mining] people pushes 'em down and they get diggin' for lumber."

His speech comes with difficulty, due to partial paralysis of his face and shortage of breath. Frequently during the conversation we take time out. He wears a hearing aid. She is hanging out the wash. A small dog runs about; a few chickens peck away.

"Minin's about all the work here, outside highway work or farmin' a little. My father started workin' in the mines when he was eleven years old. I guess he was fifty-seven when he quit, he had to. He had to walk across the big mountain and it'd be late into the night when he'd come back. So we never got to see daddy but on Sunday."

JOE: I graduated from high school in 1930, November. I went to work in the mines. We worked for fifteen cents a ton. If we made a dollar and a half a day, we made pretty good money. You got up between three thirty and four in the morning. You'd start work about six. We usually got out around maybe dark or seven or eight, nine o'clock. I come back as late as ten o'clock at night. Sometimes I just laid down to sleep, not even sleep—then wash up.

I just got short-winded and just couldn't walk across the street. I'm better now than I used to be. The doctor advised me to quit work. My heart got bad to where I couldn't get enough oxygen. March of '68 I quit. They turned me down for black lung. I'm paid through Social Security. My old uncle, he retired forty-nine years old. He's been dead a long time now. Guess he had too much sand.

My hearin' . . . It coulda been affected with so much noise. I was tampin' up, shootin' the coal down, just behind the machine. I worked that continuous miner. That made lotsa noise. This hearin' aid cost me $395.

I think the United Mine Workers has let us down a little bit. I think they sold us out is what I do. They teamed up with the operators, I think.

SUSIE: I went to school with a young boy and he got mashed up in the mines. He was about eighteen years old when he got killed.

JOE: Oh, I remember lots of accidents. I guess there was eight or nine men killed while I worked at one. These truck mines I worked in was all. They wasn't union mines. The strip and the auger about got 'em all shut down right now. I have a nephew of mine run a mine. He worked about seventeen men. They all gone to unemployment now.

Yeah, I was born in an old log cabin here. I had a great-great-great-grandfather or somethin' fought that Revolution. Grandfather Fields and his brothers was in the Civil War. One on each side of it. My grandfather owned 982 acres in here. He sold his minerals [mineral rights] for twenty-seven and a half cents an acre.

You're in one of the richest areas in the world and some of the poorest people in the world. They's about twenty-eight gas and oil wells. They have one here they claim at least a three-million-dollar-a-year gas well. One of the men that works for the gas company said they valued it at twenty-five million dollars, that one well. They offered a woman seventy-five dollars on the farm that the gas well's just laid on, for destroying half an acre of her place to set that well up.

They can do that legally because they have the mineral rights—broad form deed. Eighteen eighty-nine, my grandfather sold this, everything known and all that might be found later—gas, oil, coal, clay, stone . . . My grandfather and grandmother signed it with two X's. They accepted the farmin' rights. Company can dig all your timber, all your soil off, uncover everything, just to get their coal. Go anywhere they want to, drill right in your garden if they want to.

They took bulldozers and they tore the top off the ground. I couldn't plow it or nothin' where they left it. Come through right by that walnut tree. I've got corn this year, first year I raised it. About four years since they left. Nice corn over there. I had to move a lot of rock where they took the bulldozers.

They threatened my wife with trespassin' here because she called up the water pollution man, the gas and oil company did. (Laughs.) If the oil runs down this creek, it'd kill the fish and everything in it. And I had a lot of chickens to die, too, from drinkin' that oil.

SUSIE: When they come through with them bulldozers and tear it up like that, the dirt from it runs down to our bottom land and it ruins the water. Our drinkin' water gets muddy. So we don't have much of a chance, don't look like.

Our boy in the Navy when he comes back, he says all he can see is the mountain tore up with bulldozers. Even the new roads they built, they's debris on it and you can't hardly get through it sometimes. I guess that's what they send our boys off to fight for, to keep 'em a free country and then they do to us like that. Nothin' we can do about it. He said it was worse here than it was over in Vietnam. Four times he's been in Vietnam. He said this was a worse toreup place than Vietnam. He said, "What's the use of goin' over there an' fightin' and then havin' to come back over here an' pay taxes on somethin' that's torn up like that?"

JOE: If we don't organize together, why these big companies is just gonna take anything they want. That's the only chance on earth we got. It's all gone over to the rich man. Even the President. And we don't have a governor.

Susie: Everybody talk about it all the time. Especially Aunt Katherine up here, that's all me an' her talk about—what they done to us. My mother and father sold all their land out, where my mother's buried. Company said they sold the mineral to some other company and they was goin' to auger it. They won't have to dig the holes for the ones if they're goin' into my mother's grave. 'Cause there won't be enough left of 'em to dig a hole for. We're not gonna let it happen to my mother's grave because there's seven of us children and I know that five of us will stay right there and see that they don't do that.

They said, men from the company, we'd get a road up to the cemetery that's on top of the hill. I said, "Well, it won't be any use goin' up there, because there won't be any dead up there. There'll just be tombstones settin' there. Because the coal is under the graves." An old preacher down there, they augered under the grave where his wife is buried. And he's nearly blind and he prayed an' everything.

It's something to think about, that a man to make a few dollars would go through and under a cemetery like that. Not even respecting the dead. You can't talk to 'em. They won't talk to you about it. They walk off and leave you. They know they're doin' wrong.

Our son just come back from Vietnam, he went to work for a strip mine. We told him we wouldn't allow him to work for them and stay home. So he quit. He was tellin' me yesterday, looks like he's gonna have to go back to work. I said, "Well, do you want me to pack your clothes tonight or do you want to wait until morning to get 'em? 'Cause," I said, "when you start workin' for the strip mines, you're not comin' back here. I'm not responsible for anything that happens to ya." Don't want none of ours in that, no way.

You and Joe have very little money. Life is rough and life is hard . . . Your son could pick up about fifty dollars a day . . .

SUSIE: From forty-five to eighty a day.

JOE: He's an equipment operator.

SUSIE: Yeah, he worked and he made good. But we didn't want him in that. He was gonna get killed over there and we wouldn't be responsible for no doctor bills and no funeral bills for him—if he was gonna do that kind of work. Then he said he had to make a livin' some way. Well, he's gonna have to go back to the army, look like. I said, "Go to the army and come back. Maybe you can get a job then." He said he didn't want to go to the army. And he went to work for one of his cousins, night watchin'. He makes $150 a week. But he told me yesterday that they were gonna close down over there and he was gonna have to go back and work for the strip mines. I said, "When you start work, I'll pack your clothes. You're not gonna stay here."

We sent him to school for him to take this heavy equipment. I worked and cooked over at the school, helped send him there. I said, "I'm not sendin' you to school to come out here and go to work for these strip mines." I'd rather see him in Vietnam than see him doin' strip jobs.

I just think if it's not stopped by officials and governor and all, we're just gonna have to take guns and stop it. When they come to your land . . . We got tax receipts here dated back to 1848 that the Haynes and Fields paid tax on this place. Do you think we should let some money grabber come here and destroy it? For nothin'? And have to move out?

JOE: They sweated my grandfathers out of it. Millions of dollars . . .

SECOND CHANCE: FRED RINGLEY [5]

We have a small farm in Arkansas. It's a mile and a half off the highway on a dirt road on top of a hill. It's thirteen and a half acres. We call it Lucky Thirteen. We are in the process of building a cattle herd, because you can't make a living as a farmer unless you have thousands of acres.

We have five children, six to eleven. Three girls and two boys. The eleven-year-old boy takes care of the cattle. The ten-year-old girl takes care of the chickens. The nine-year-old boy takes care of the two hogs. And the youngest girls takes care of the dog.

We purchased a dairy bar—a combination ice cream parlor and hamburger joint. My wife and I alternate from ten in the morning until ten at night. This is a carry-out joint. It's a mama-and-papa operation. A Benedictine abbey sits on top of the hill. It's a boarding school for boys. They don't like the food in their dining room and they furnish our daytime business.

He is forty years old. Until a year ago he had lived all his life in the environs of Chicago. He was born in one of its North Shore suburbs; he was raised, reached adulthood, and became a paterfamilias *as a "typical suburbanite." His was a bedroom community, middle-class, "of struggle for the goods of the world." He had worked in advertising as a copywriter and salesman.*

We were caught up in the American Dream. You've gotta have a house. You've gotta have a country club. You've gotta have two cars. Here you are at ten grand and getting nowhere. So I doubled my salary. I also doubled my grief. I now made twenty thousand dollars, had an expense account, a Country Squire—air conditioned station wagon

[5] From *Working: People Talk About What They Do All Day, and How They Feel About What They Do*, by Studs Terkel, reporter and interviewer. Pantheon Books. '74. p. 532–7. Copyright © 1972, 1974 by Studs Terkel. Reprinted by permission of Pantheon Books, a division of Random House, Inc.

given by the company—a wonderful boss. We began to accumulate. We got a house in the suburbs and we got a country club membership and we got two cars and we got higher taxes. We got nervous and we started drinking more and smoking more. Finally, one day we sat down. We have everything and we are poor.

The superhighways were coming through. Ramada Inn moved in and Holiday Inn moved in. We used to sit around until three in the morning my wife and I, and say, "There's gotta be a better way." We own a travel trailer. We said, "Suppose we hook the trailer up to the car and just went around these United States and tried to figure out where would be a good place to live—where we could make a living and still have the natural background we want. How could we do it? We're only average people. We don't put any money away. Our equity is in our home."

We sold the house, paid off everybody we owe, put our furniture in storage, and started driving. We had everything in the big city and quit while we were still ahead. We had seen what we wanted to see in the East. It's time to go West.

We had two criteria: water and climate. We ruled out the North and the deep South. That left us a straight line from Indianapolis to New Mexico. We decided central Arkansas was the best for environment. They've backed up the river and made these fantastic lakes. We bought this farm.

Our neighbors came over. They're sixty-eight. They're broiler farmers.* She plays piano in the church, by songbooks written in do-re-mi notes. I brought a record out—hits of the last sixty years. It was from Caruso to Mario Lanza or something. She didn't recognize one piece of music on that

* "Arkansas is the leading producer of poultry in the United States. The broiler farmer invests somewhere between twenty and thirty thousand dollars in two chicken houses. They hold up to seven thousand baby chicks. The packing company puts the chicks in and supplies the feed and medicine. At the end of eight weeks they're four and a half pounds. The companies pick 'em up and pay you for 'em. Ralph Nader's been after them. It's almost white slavery. The farmer invests and the company can say, 'This is a lousy lot, we're not gonna pay you the full price.' But you're still putting in twelve hours a day."

record except Eddy Arnold. They didn't get a radio down there until about 1950, because they weren't wired for electricity.† So we've got one foot in the thirties and one in the seventies.

We have a milk cow, a Jersey. I had never put my hand on a cow. The people we bought the home from taught us how to milk her. We discovered a cow can be contrary and hold her milk up if she wants to tighten certain muscles and doesn't like your cold grip. People would come over and watch us and laugh.

All through this eight-thousand-mile trip, Daddy is thinking, Maybe I haven't done the right thing. Everywhere I went, they said, "You'll never make money." Friends said, "Oh, Fred's lost his beans." We were digging into our backlog money for food. Time was passing. It was winter.

I realize there are only two ways to do things: work for somebody else or be an owner. There are two classes of people, the haves and the have-nots. The haves own. I went to the local bank and discovered that this dairy bar was for sale. I said, "I can cook a hamburger." But I'd never worked in a restaurant, even as a bus boy or a soda jerk. We borrowed a hundred percent of the money from the bank, fourteen thousand dollars. We revamped the entire place because it hadn't been kept up.

We don't have car hops. You come to the window. We serve you a to-go meal through the window. Inside we have five tables, and in the alcove a little game room with three pinball machines. We serve hamburger, fried chicken, pizzaburger—we introduced it in the area—chili dogs, Tastee

† Clyde Ellis, a former congressman from Arkansas, recalls, "I wanted to be at my parents' house when electricity came. It was in 1940. We'd all go around flipping the switch, to make sure it hadn't come on yet. We didn't want to miss it. When they finally came on, the lights just barely glowed. I remember my mother smiling. When they came on full, tears started to run down her cheeks. After a while she said: 'Oh, if only we had it when you children were growing up.' We had lots of illness. Anyone who's never been in a family without electricity—with illness—can't imagine the difference. . . . They had all kinds of parties—mountain people getting light for the first time. There are still areas without electricity . . ." —Quoted in Studs Terkel's *Hard Times*. Pantheon Books, 1970.

Freeze, candy. Bubble gum's a good seller. We sell a plastic bag of shaved ice for a quarter to tourists, fishermen. Coke, Dr. Pepper, Sprite. Fish sandwiches.

We've had the bar only six months. We're trying to get it to a point where we spend less and less time there. The owner has to be there, 'cause they come in to see you as much as they come in to eat. They come in and say, "How's the cow?" They've never forgotten. They say, "How's the farm and how are the ticks?" And so on. And, "The place looks nice." They get all dressed up for this. The wife puts on her best dress and comes to the dairy bar for dinner. It's a big deal.

If all goes well and we've doubled the business, we'll close when school closes. Maybe we'll close for Easter week. And then close another week when the boys in the abbey have off. So we'll end with a month's vacation. We're only a day's drive from New Orleans. We'll go there this winter.

My wife opens the place at ten. Help comes from eleven to one—high school girls. At three she comes home and gets me. We traded our Country Squire for a used pickup truck. At about three thirty the boys come from the abbey and play pinball machines and have hamburgers. I stay until ten at night.

I'm a short order cook and bottle washer and everything else—until ten. Shut the lights off, clean the grill. Sometimes I'll stop off at the tavern across the street and shoot the breeze until he closes at eleven. I'll come home and my wife is watching the news or Johnny Carson. That's when we talk. She tells me how the animals are doing and the kids are doing. We go to bed about midnight and it starts all over the next day. Except Monday.

Monday we're closed. Now we begin to reap the benefits of what we went there for. On Monday we put the kids on the bus to school. We get in the truck, we throw the boat in the back. Six minutes from our front door, we put it in one of the world's largest man-made lakes and go fishing and picnicking and mess around until four o'clock when the kids come home. We sit out there, where I don't suppose three boats go by us all day long. Sit and watch the copperheads on the shore and the birds overhead. Discussing Nixon and Daley and fishing and the dairy bar and whatever. What's astonishing is we can climb a mountain right across from our home. There's a waterfall at the top. And no jets going over. No people. Just a pickup truck down the road now and then.

A man stood on Eden's Highway (an expressway leading into and out of Chicago) and took a survey of guys driving to work. Their jaw muscles were working. I was one of those guys. I was this guy with his eyes bulging and swearing and saying, "You rotten guy, get out of my way." For what? So I could get to work to get kicked around by a purchasing agent because his job is five minutes late? That forty-five minutes' drive to work. I would usually have about five cigarettes. Constant close calls, jam-ups, running late, tapping the foot on the floor, thumping that wheel, and everything that everybody does.

I would get to the office. You might find the paper hadn't been delivered, the press had broken down, the boss might be in a foul mood. Or you might have a guy on the phone screaming that he had to see you in half an hour or else the whole world would end. They always had to have an estimate first. So you'd do your paper work as fast as you could. Then you'd start your round of daily calls. Then came the hassle for parking space. Are you lucky enough to get one of those hour jobs on the street or do you go in the lot? If you go in the lot, what're they gonna do to your car before they give it back to you? How many dents? So you go through that hassle.

Then it would be lunch time. You'd take a guy to lunch, have two or three drinks. Rich food . . . You come out of the darkened restaurant back into the summer afternoon. At four you'd take whatever jobs you had assembled or proofs you had to look over. Maybe work until five thirty or six. Then you're fighting the traffic back to the suburb.

I'd be home at a quarter to seven. We would just sit down and eat. We would finish at eight, with dinner and conversation, looking at the kids' report cards and whatever. Then we'd watch TV if something decent was on. If it was daylight saving time, we'd play ball with the kids until nine or ten. Then we'd go to bed. Or else we'd start hacking away at our personal problems. Mostly it was fighting the bills. On weekends we'd go to the country club for dinner. I belonged for three years and never played the course. I never had time.

Just the intolerable strain of living here is fantastic, especially when you've been away for a year. I haven't been as nervous in one day driving mountains with radiators blowing out as I was the half-hour it took my father to drive me down here this morning—in his Oldsmobile.

If you decide to cut and run, you've got to do it in one clean break. You'll never do it if you piddle away and if you wait until you're sixty. A fellow I know, he was sixty-three, bought a piece of land in Taos, on a mountain top, forty acres. He and his wife were gonna go in three years and move there. He told me this on a Tuesday. On Saturday his wife was dead in the garden. The day he buried her he said to me, "Boy, you're so smart to get out while you're young." Our decision to make this journey evolved over a period of years. Not so strangely, it came about with our achievement of what is called the American Dream.

People say, "You're wasting your college education." My ex-employer said to my father, "You didn't raise your son to be a hash slinger." I've lost status in the eyes of my big city friends. But where I am now I have more status than I would in the city. I'm a big fish in a little pond. I'm a minor celebrity. I can be a hash slinger there and be just as fine as the vice president of the Continental Bank. If I were a hash slinger in the suburbs, they'd ask me to move out of the neighborhood. I said to myself as a kid, What's Mr. So-and-so do? Oh, he only runs a cleaners. He's not a big wheel at all. My personal status with somebody else may have gone down. My personal status with myself has gone up a hundred percent.

I think an education is to make you well-rounded. The first room we built in this house was the library. But I believe we've gotten too far away from physical work. I found this out working around my house in the suburb. I could have one terrible day and come home and hang a wall of wallpaper and get so involved, do the edges, make sure there are no air bubbles under it—that I could forget all my frustrations. I don't think jogging is enough. I believe most suburban guys are happier and easier to get along with when they're out cutting the grass than when they're in that Cadillac. I work on the house in Arkansas. It's just an old oak frame. There's no finish. I'm remodeling all the way through. You're rehanging doors and moving thresholds. Just by trial and error. When I walked out of my old life I weighed 185 pounds. As you see me today I weigh 160. I feel healthier than I've ever felt in my life.

I don't say I'm gonna end up the rest of my life as a hash slinger, either. I may buy more land and get more involved in cattle. I would like to go a hundred percent in farming, but it would require ten times the land I've got, and it takes time . . . In the cattle business there's enough demand for meat, so you can make a comfortable living between the cattle and the broilers. I might expand the dairy bar into a regular restaurant, make it a little fancy. I've got a lot of different ways to go.

But one thing we've still got—the one thing my wife would not let me get rid of—is we still got the trailer. We can go again if we have to. If we found something better, maybe a higher mountain top to live on, we'd go live there.

BIBLIOGRAPHY

An asterisk (*) preceding a reference indicates that the article or a part of it has been reprinted in this book.

BOOKS AND PAMPHLETS

* Allen, F. L. Since yesterday. Harper. '39.

Barnes, Peter, ed. The people's land; a reader on land reform in the U.S.; ed. for the National Coalition for Land Reform. Rodale Press. '75.
   Review. Progressive. 39:57-8. O. '75. Larry Lack.

Baum, Patricia. Another way of life: the story of communal living. Putnam. '73.

Beame, Hugh and others. Home comfort: stories and scenes of life on Total Loss Farm; ed. by Richard Wizansky. Saturday Review Press. '73.

Beard, C. A. Economic origins of Jeffersonian democracy. Macmillan. '27.

Bestor, A. E. Backwoods utopias; the sectarian and Owenite phases of communitarian socialism in America, 1663-1829. University of Pennsylvania Press. '50.

Booth, E. T. Country life in America. Greenwood. '73.

Borsodi, Ralph. Flight from the city: an experiment in creative living on the land. Harper. '72.
   Originally published in 1933.

* Brogan, D. W. Politics in America. Harper. '54; (Anchor Books) Doubleday. paper ed. '60.

Bussey, E. M. The flight from rural poverty—how nations cope. Lexington Books. '73.

Chamber of Commerce of the United States. The changing structure of U.S. agribusiness and its contributions to the national economy. The Organization. 1615 H St. N.W. Washington, D.C. 20006. '74.

* Clemens, S. L. Life on the Mississippi; with biographical illustrations and drawings from the first edition of the book together with an introduction by Guy A. Cardwell. Dodd. ['68?]
   Originally published in 1883.

* Clemens, S. L. Mark Twain's autobiography. Harper. '24. 2v.

Cobb, Betsy and Cobb, Hubbard. City people's guide to country living. Macmillan. '73.

Cohen, Daniel. Not of this world: a history of the commune in America. Follett. '74.

Coles, Robert. The South goes north. Little, Brown. '71.

Farb, Peter. Living earth. Harper. '59.

Follett, Muriel. New England year: a journal of Vermont farm life. Gale. '71.

Garland, Hamlin. A son of the middle border. 10th ptg Macmillan. '61.

Gibbons, Euell. Stalking the healthful herbs. McKay. '66.

Gibbons, Euell. Stalking the wild asparagus. McKay. '62.

Gordon, Michael, ed. Nuclear family in crisis: the search for an alternative. Harper. '72.

Halpern, J. M. The changing village community. Prentice-Hall. '67.

Higbee, E. C. Farms and farmers in an urban age. Twentieth Century Fund, Inc. 41 E. 70th St. New York 10021. '63.

Hightower, Jim. Hard tomatoes, hard times: the failure of the land grant college complex. Schenkman. '73.

Humphrey, H. H. War on poverty. McGraw-Hill. '64.

Johnson, G. L. and Quance, C. L. eds. The overproduction trap in U.S. agriculture. Johns Hopkins Press. '72.

Jones, G. E. Rural life: patterns and processes. Longman. '73.

Lange, Dorothea and Taylor, P. S. An American exodus: a record of human erosion. (American Farmers and the Rise of Agribusiness Series) Arno. '75.
    Reprint of 1939 edition.

* Lerner, Max. America as a civilization. Simon & Schuster. '57. 2v.

Logan, Ben. The land remembers; the story of a farm and its people. Viking. '75.

Lynd, R. S. and Lynd, H. M. Middletown, a study in contemporary American culture. Harcourt. '29.

McPhee, John. The Pine Barrens. Farrar. '68.

Melvin, B. L. and Smith, Elna. Rural youth: their situation and prospects. Da Capo Press. '71.

* Moore, T. E. The traveling man. Doubleday. '72.

National Academy of Sciences. Board on Agriculture and Renewable Resources. Agricultural production efficiency. The Academy. 2101 Constitution Ave. N.W. Washington, D.C. 20418. '75.

National Farm Institute. What's ahead for the family farm. Iowa State University Press. '66.

Nearing, Helen and Nearing, Scott. Living the good life; how to live sanely and simply in a troubled world. Schocken Books. '70.

Ogden, S. R. ed. America the vanishing: rural life and the price of progress. Greene. '69.

Ogden, Samuel. This country life. Rodale Press. '70.

Osgood, William. How to earn a living in the country without farming. Garden Way Publishing Company. '74.

Peden, Rachel. Speak to the earth. Knopf. '74.

Rexroth, Kenneth. Communalism: from its origins to the 20th century. Seabury. '75.

Richards, Eugene. Few comforts or surprises: the Arkansas delta. MIT Press. '73.

* Rourke, Constance. American humor. Harcourt. '31.

Russell, S. P. The farm: how people live and work on the farm. Parents' Magazine Press. '70.

Saloutos, Theodore and Hicks, J. D. Twentieth-century populism; agricultural discontent in the Middle West, 1900-1939. University of Nebraska Press. '64.
  Originally published with title: Agricultural discontent in the Middle West, 1900-1939.

Schlebecker, J. T. Whereby we thrive: a history of American farming 1607-1972. Iowa State University Press. '75.

Seim, R. K. The American farmer. Rand McNally College Publishing Company. '74.

Simons, A. M. The American farmer. (American Farmers and the Rise of Agribusiness Series) Arno. '75.
  Reprint of 1903 edition.

Stadfield, C. K. From the land and back. Scribner. '74.

Steinbeck, John. The grapes of wrath. Viking. '39.

Strachan, Bill, ed. Foxfire two. Doubleday. '75.

Strachan, Bill, ed. Foxfire three. Doubleday. '75.

Taylor, C. C. The farmers' movement, 1620-1920. American Book. '53.

* Terkel, Studs. Working: people talk about what they do all day, and how they feel about what they do. Pantheon Books. '74.

* Thoreau, H. D. Walden and other writings; ed. with an introd. by Brooks Atkinson. (Modern Library College Editions) Random House. '50.

* Tocqueville, Alexis de. Democracy in America. Knopf. '45. 2v.
  Originally published in 1835.

United States. Congress. Senate. Agriculture and Forestry Committee. Transportation in rural America: interim report, analysis of current crisis in rural transportation prepared by Economic Research Service. 93d Congress, 2d Session. Supt. of Docs. Washington, D.C. 20402. '74.

United States. Department of Agriculture. Farmers in a changing world; yearbook of agriculture, 1940. (House Document No. 695) 76th Congress, 3d Session. Supt. of Docs. Washington, D.C. 20402. '40.

Wigginton, Eliot, ed. The Foxfire book: hog dressing; log cabin building; mountain crafts and foods; planting by signs; snake lore, hunting tales, faith healing; moonshining; and other affairs of plain living. Doubleday. '72.

* Wilson, C. M. Backwoods America. University of North Carolina Press. '34.

Wilson, C. M. Country living; plus and minus. Stephen Daye Press. '38.

Wilson, C. M. Roots: miracles below. Doubleday. '68.

Woodson, C. G. Rural Negro. Greene. '75.

Periodicals

Business Week. p 52. S. 22, '75. Agriculture's need: for $400-billion.

Current. 170:36-41. F. '75. State of U.S. agriculture. Wilson Clark.

Department of State Bulletin. 73:453-4. S. 22, '75. President praises agriculture's role in economy and world peace; remarks, August 18, 1975. G. R. Ford.

Environment. 17:4-5. Jl. '75. Price of monopoly: marketing cooperatives and marketing orders. K. P. Shea.

Farm Journal. 99:66. F. '75. Profits aren't obscene.

Farm Journal. 99:16-17. Je. '75. Who says we're out of land? First colony farms. Lane Palmer.

Farm Journal. 99:N2. O. '75. What farmers can—and can't—get in Washington. R. D. Wennblom.

Farm Journal. 100:N4. Ja. '76. Farm women press for tax reform. Laura Lane.

Farm Journal. 100:56-7. Ja., 50-1. F., 40. mid-F., 58. Mr., 50. Ap. '76. Farm people.

Farm Journal. 100:18. mid-F. '76. Farmers who do their own exporting.

* Farm Journal. 100:24-6+. F. '76. American farmer . . . our first "hybrid." R. C. Black.

Farm Journal. 100:30. Ap. '76. Food marketing costs: bulging faster.

Fortune. 86:134-9+. Ag. '72. Corporate farming: a tough row to hoe. Dan Cordtz.

Futurist. 9:196-202. Ag. '75. Renewed growth in rural communities. C. L. Beale.

* Futurist. 9:202-4. Ag. '75. The new ruralism: the post-industrial age is upon us. W. N. Ellis.

Harper's Magazine. 250:7. Mr. '75. Prodigality and fatted calves. O. L. Staley.

Harvard Business Review. 53:81-95. My. '75. U.S. agribusiness breaks out of isolation. R. A. Goldberg.

Intellect. 103:211. Ja. '75. Agriculture, finance, and inflation.

Intellect. 104:81-2. S. '75. Urbanization of agriculture by year 2000.

Ms. 4:22. N. '75. Over here: the Women's Land Army; farmerettes. Anita Voorhees.

New York Post. p 37. Mr. 10, p 41. Mr. 12, '76. The peons of Florida. Jack Anderson and Les Whitten.

New York Post. p 27. Mr. 13, '76. Poverty in the fields. Jack Anderson and Les Whitten.

New York Times. p 33. Ag. 14, '75. Under new rules, what was a farm may no longer be.

* New York Times. sec IV, p 2. Ag. 17, '75. America's rural poor: the picture is changing. Jon Nordheimer.

New York Times. p 1+. D. 12, '75. 85% of rise in population found in South and West. Robert Reinhold.

New York Times Magazine. p 14-16+. F. 29, '76. Looking for: a new world. D. R. Pellman.

Organic Gardening and Farming. 22:42-6. S. '75. Rural renaissance on the way [editorial]. Robert Rodale.

* Organic Gardening and Farming. 22:128-31. N. '75. The keys to homesteading success. Gene Logsdon.

Organic Gardening and Farming. 23:58-62. F. '76. Small is necessary [views of E. F. Schumacher and Nicholas Georgescu-Roegen]. Robert Rodale.

Ramparts. 13:34-7+. Jl. '75. Marketplace of hunger. Susan De-Marco and Susan Sechler.

* St. Louis Globe Democrat. Ap. '89. Settling Oklahoma.

Science. 188:434-6. My. 2, '75. Crop forecasting from space: toward a global flood watch. A. L. Hammond.

* Science. 188:531-4. My. 9, '75. U.S. agribusiness and agricultural trends. John Walsh.

Science News. 107:302-3. My. 10, '75. Food: a good moment for stocktaking.

Successful Farming. 73:7-10. Ja. '75. New economics of farming. Richard Krumme.

Successful Farming. 73:no2 9. F. '75. Incorporate or pay up: effects of Financial amendment act of 1974. Richard Krumme.

Successful Farming. 73:no4 9. Mr. '75. Consulting: time for college to own up.

Successful Farming. 73:B4-5. Ap. '75. Whip farm grime with power cleaners. Bob Thies.

Successful Farming. 73:23-33. Je. '75. Marketing: the last void in farming; symposium.

Successful Farming. 73:19-21. Ag. '75. Starting over; moving to new farms. Bill Gergen.

Successful Farming. 73:9. N. '75. Farm sociology, economics not compatible.

Successful Farming. 73:9. N. '75. Farmer co-ops try competing with big grain companies.

Successful Farming. 73:29. N. '75. Business organization.

U.S. News & World Report. 79:26-7. Jl. 28, '75. Basic facts about a key industry.

Vital Speeches of the Day. 41:724-8. S. 15, '75. Emerging partnership of coal and agriculture; coal production and utilization; address, August 20, 1975, C. E. Bagge.